AHEAD

OF

POVERTY

"A CURABLE DISEASE THAT NEEDS SPECIAL ATTENTION"

ADETOPE ADENIJI

DEDICATION

The book is dedicated to the Almighty God, the knowledge of the world.

Also, to my biological parent, The Very Rev.and late Mrs.J.A. Adeniji (RTD).

And my father and mentor; Sir A.B.A. Aladekomo.

TABLE OF CONTENT

ACKNOWLEDGEMENT

My appreciations to my wife Tope Adeniji, son, Tomiwa and daughter, Adedamola.

My biological parents and mentor; The Very Rev.&Mrs.J.A.Adeniji

My father and mother/mentor; Sir &Mrs.A.B.A. Aladekomo.

And fathers;Daddy&Mummy Dipo Komolafe, Daddy &late Mrs.Ayo Oni, Engr&Mrs.Lana Odutola, and host of the others.

To my siblings and all relative; thank you for your constant support.

To all my friends and amiable; thank you exceedingly.

My church; Methodist Church Nigeria, most especially, Wesley Chapel Lekki, Lagos and the entire churches in the whole universe, I say thank you.

To all other religion bodies where the knowledge of peace, love and undiluted coexistence is being preached, I say thank you.

Lastly; appreciation to all the teachers in all cadre and categories; You are the best and the most noted in term of your effort to design lives.

Thank you all and God bless you all.

Tope Adeniji

INTRODUCTION

Poverty is a common word that intimidates the lazy and lackadaisical minded individual because of their inaction to be in control of the situation that has made them to be less privileged. It erupts as a result of the prevailing situation that does not permit a lasting solution to the menaces that make the human being not to have the permissible effort to create a unique attention and control on the issues.

The issue of the inequality around the globe of the world has made most of the artificial causes of the hardship that have led to the massive poverty. To be poor does not mean that one does not have anything in his pocket or to eat at the point of evaluating him, but it means the state of hopelessness that emerges as a result of not having any confidence in tomorrow.

There is none that has not been put into one condition or the other at a point or the other, but the nature of the solution catered for each circumstance are what made them a futuristic benefits or living in a deplorable state consistently.

There is no one that is not equipped to the tune of gaining full control over the issues around him. It might be very difficult and very uneasy to have a way ahead, but the mind set to function under the auction to attain the stage of higher living standard is pertinent to gain full control on what it takes to break the yoke of poverty.

Some refer to their effort contributed to the reality at the point of moving up or growing up to attain their desire as part of the substances that could be ascribed to be poverty, but reverse is the case. The act of adding value to oneself can never be poverty irrespective of the condition that one passed through at the time of doing so. What connects a man to the internal potency to step into the action that can lead out of the poverty can never be attributed to be poverty but measures to create future. The argument is that, whatever you pass through at the moment of adjusting your pathway to success can never be apportioned to be poverty but rather what empowers you to take a lead in eradicating and adjusting poverty.

Poverty is always ashamed and frighten of the creativity and hardworking. It is never what can be afflicted with the disciplined minded and mental alertness minded individuals, and the sets of the individuals that are always resilient to make contribution. It is a condition that erupt as a result of nonchalant attitude often, but that can be cured permanently when the full attention is gratifies to its nullification.

Quite pathetic and uninteresting to the height of no honour to understand that the little babies now understand better of the definitions of the poverty before they commence their lives, most of the new born babies are born dominated with the poverty which does not allow them to realize that it is never a must to live in it. There is no way one will not realize the need to be in charge and he will be in control of the situations around his destiny. More insight can be extracted from my book" Take Charge".

Quite shameful that the government do not actually realize that they are failing in their part to create an enabling environment and facilities that should make the masses or the populace to have all it takes to have a taste of life, and the populace do not often get to know what their desire and want in term of the social amenities and infrastructures should come like, and mostly, they even have no interest on agitating for their desire and wants.

One of the most uninteresting circumstances that has enveloped most of the human nature is attributed to the instance of poverty, whereby the set of the individuals living in it do not realize the need to be responsible for its eradication, while the populace remain calm and quite, believing that the state at which they are is the best suited to them or assigned by the nature of their destiny.

When the nature of the education and exposure that should formulate the internal decision is absolutely absent in the growing techniques and technicalities of the growing human, at a point in time when the white collar jobs are limited, graduates become the carrier of abject poverty and find it very complex to create a life of their own. To grow with the nature of the environment that should create future and enabling provision on constant basis, there is need of the creativity to be in surplus to meet with the demand of the present time and the time to come.

Without making findings on the way out of the poverty and to know what are responsible for it, there might not be any need to have a remedy to it. However, when one can not find a lasting solution to his predicaments or associated issues around his life, he might never be able to extend life to another man. Any life lived without having a meaningful effect on the others is a life lived wasted.

There must be separation between living to fulfill destiny and living in poverty never to be ashamed to give out all what it takes to reclaim purpose and destiny. When you can strife for a way out, as I said, irrespective of sorrowful nature or disdain structure you pass through, you will still definitely be above the poverty. But reversely, when you have lost the control and the foresight to move out of the menace created by the poverty or you have no option other than receiving the condition as it may come, then, the poverty exists and lives to abject in nature which means that in such situation, one get glorifies with the abnormality.

There must be thorough analysis that should encourage the younger ones to understand better of the intrinsic connotation of what poverty means, to know when they are setting for the corrective and amendment or compounding the situation around them.

The book "ahead of poverty" will certainly reveal the full definition of poverty, the causes, nature of poverty and at the end, there will be placement and enumeration of the reasonable way out. Kindly read through my thought in concern with the logics to make an expensive illustration that can be a catalyst to the economic advancement and general betterment.

Tope Adeniji

Abuja,Nigeria.

West Africa.

+2348037184404/+2348080935806

CHAPTER (ONE)

<u>POVERTY</u>

In this very particular chapter, there will be need to study adversely the meaning of the poverty, to be able to have a perfect definition and interpretation that can give the full clue on the whole logics behind the word.

Poverty can be accessed intentionally or carelessly, and it can be an attraction or influence. What this means is that poverty is made to be part of one's life as a result of being careless in the reasoning, thought or action. It is not inflicted or considered to be inflicted. Poverty can be constructed base on the intentional act of the people. So also, it can be an attraction, which means it can be emulated based on what one sees. It also emanates as a result of being influenced by the factors around the situation surrounding one's destiny.

What is poverty? Poverty means not having money for the basic needs such as food, drinking water, shelter or toilets. It is the state of being extremely poor. It is the state of being inferior in quality or insufficient in amount. These are the definition extracted from the dictionary and lexicon I could lay my hands on at the moment of writing this book.

However, to get directly involved with my conceptual thought and ideology as regards the context of the book, I will define poverty as the condition that limit or does not permit someone to see possibilities. What this means is that, when someone find it very difficult to see the need to have the corrective measures on the hardship in which he lives, he lives in poverty.

It can be termed to be the nature of suppression and hardship that makes one to live under bondage and suffering of the aftermath result of poverty. This means that, it has to do with the forces that can not be seen or that are abstract which control the innate man not to turn off the difficult situation they are or living in. it means that though the condition was not tolerable or conducive, the forces make one to be very comfortable with the irritating condition without seeing any need to complain or to have a reasonable change.

It can be defined as a situation at which one does not see beyond the condition or situation that the hardship had put him. Here, I meant that when one's thinking faculty is not above the immediate condition in which one lives, it turns to be penury and poverty. A man should see the essentiality of being outside of the condition he has found himself, and that is the only avenue to see the need to have solution to the issues and at the same time to be inclined with the technicalities that can be the solution to the poverty issues.

One can define poverty as the inability to have conviction in the solution to the desirable desires. This means that when one does not have what it entails to be convinced as regards the solution to the desirable desires, he lives in the poverty. To live above poverty, there must be zeal to act and to be able to see the work being involved with creating an atmosphere of relief. There must be conviction and absolute interest in the remedy to be given or planned to attack the nature of the hardship one is involved.

Poverty means living a clueless nature of life. A clueless life can be a nature of life that is of no purpose and indifference to the situation. It is when one had concluded that the nature of his life is attributable to his generational or antecedent issues, and there can not be control that can be offered or given anymore. This is option to the hopefulness. It is when one can not see any reason to cause a translation or convert deficiency to efficiency or his advantage.

Poverty can be defined in term of material substance and other nature of the other things that are not available at the point they are needed or can not be accessed when due. Such situagtion is termed poverty. When there is no financial viability to meet with the desires in connection with the material substance and other relative things that might be essential to life related issues, it might mean poverty. To live a life above poverty, there must be resources that are enough or sufficient to meet the demand of time when due not only ordinarily, but to derive the utmost value and enjoyment of what they should offer. When there is urge to buy a cloth and the cloth can not be bought at when due or to meet up with the desire and the intention; the gap between the time of need and the time of being able to get such materials as a result of lack of financial capability can measure the poverty level sometimes.

Inability to make difference in one's environment is termed poverty. Each individual is meant to be a catalyst to the bliss of change and to have something worthwhile to be given to the society. Unlike the thought of many individuals that money answers everything. I am not disputing on what money can do or its effects in the world, but I only want us to know that having something other than money to offer indirectly means money in its measurement monetarily. Therefore, being not involved either directly or indirectly on making impact can be termed to be poverty.

It can be termed to be a situation whereby mental efficacy and rational thought are not the concern of the order of living. When one can not see the reason to have an in-depth thought and rational concern for the things in line with the existence, he lives in poverty. To live above poverty, one must be able to live a life with full intellectual contents to make decision and values that can improve the efficacy of the functions around the world. It means logicality and intellectual power that has to do with the level of living.

It means an attitude that accepts what the nature got to offer. I deliberated on a point similar to this at the earlier stage. The inability to make a move or relate on the action that should lead one beyond the state of stagnancy or odds condition that one found oneself is termed poverty. Poverty is not what can not be corrected or changed, but the condition can only be changed when there is provision for the changes. Therefore, a man must never be too mindful of the disability in the ability to gain full control of the situation of his life.

It means not thinking above the material and monetary values of money. The implication of this is that, the major concern are centered on the need of the money not those things that are related to the causes of the poverty. Many nations are inclusive in the aspect just mentioned, due to their inability to understand the trick to overcome it. The monetary and material values are created by something, and when it is not thoroughly created and adequately provided, they are converted to hardship and pains that lead to the state of penury and poverty. There must be constant need to develop one's interest, that is much more greater than just the value of money.

Poverty is referred to as the disability that is caused by one's decision or indecision and the reaction of one to correct it or not. Poverty is what is caused by wrong doings often, and sometimes, things that one considers right due to the limited of the understanding. There is never any issue in having difficulties or moving through difficulties, but there is always issue in connection to the reaction of men not attempting to resolve them. Some individuals consider issue created to be the determinant of their lives, while they fail to take the necessary action to bring about the relevant solution. Poverty is referred to as the disability and the weakness of not having the solution to the irregular standard of living.

To have a perception that poverty is not curable is termed poverty. The state of mind is very essential at the point of measuring the nature and standard of poverty. A mind that can not think or reason above poverty might not be able to have a solution to it. Proffering solution to the nature of hardship or poor standard of the living condition entails reasonability. One might never be able to have what he can not see, one must see the need to accomplish the adjustment around the situation he passes through before he can attain the stage of its correction. The power of thought is relevant to the nature of conclusion and end result. Therefore, to have the best of the greatest solution to the prevailing poverty ravaging the world, there must be perception that can be of advantage to the improvement of the standard that can be accessed.

One can term poverty as the tools and materials that introduce riches, solution and foresight to the populace. Sometimes, without the condition that is meant to be resolved, there might never be any consideration to resolve or put an end to them. There must be something that triggers the urge to have movement to the ending of a particular nature of issue. Without the full experience of some certain things in life, there will never be the need to give attention them.

What has happened in life is quite very essential to the reaction and solution to be generated by the people, but what is happening is far more exclusively related to the appropriate determinant of the final solution. The intellectual structure of the human being has made them to know things that are right from the one that are wrong. There are many natural things that are considered right at a time, which at the end turns out to be wrong when well considered or as a result of the defects created by them or the adjustment that should be taken on them.

To sight an example, the land reclamation of the Atlantic Ocean or other kinds of reclamation is worth to be given a thought. This is a situation whereby the land or space occupies by the ocean, seas and other stagnant or moving water is sound filled for the use of the human pedestrian and economic functionality. What I am trying to point out is that poverty is the cause of having the notion that makes one not to have a transcending nature of thought to overcome. However, with the fact that poverty is a source of misfortune and hardship, its nature also initiate the riches, betterment, foresight and the required solution which count to be an added advantage to the humanitarian advancement.

These sets of the interpretation are however of greater value to the idea of the content of the poverty as connected with the book" ahead of poverty". There will definitely be other relative terms and words that will definitely say more on what poverty means, but they will definitely be well illustrated and adequately elucidated to understand them fully.

CHAPTER (TWO)

<u>POVERTY IS CAUSED NOT AFFLICTED</u>

Having the clue on the causes of the poverty is very relevant to have the best of the solution to the menace. Poverty is caused not afflicted. The statement is a logical expression illustrating the cause of the poverty. Some believe that the causes are rested on the spiritual nature of the forces that strive with the destiny, while some believe that it is in connection with the war or strenuous world that one passes through. Some believe that poverty is in association with the nature of the forces that are related with the family antecedent related issues or curses that are generational in nature. I have not written to nullify the instances that are in correlation with our lineage of thought as Africans, but I want to create a better logic towards having a winning edge on all sorts in any nature that are created.

Thinking on the causes of poverty to the nature of the instances I have mentioned is more killing compares to the poverty itself. What one is not afraid of effect of hardship; there might never be anything that can stand as limitation or hindrance on his way, but what he always count to be the problems and impediments are subjected to discomfort and poverty.

What is called poverty in not something that can be afflicted to human being and even if it is made to be taken or to be a challenge, one must never or must not accept its forces over his agenda not to flourish. A man controls things that have to do with his destiny, but when they are left to the hands of the other determinant factors, they are subjected to destruction. To move from the stage of destruction to the height of flourishing and exploring advantages, there must be understanding of how destiny works.

Your destiny is in lineage with your direction of thought and your mind set to get it turned around to come forth with the structure that can be informational and well equipped to nurture a way out.

Actually, if one fails to give it a full understanding, one can easily attribute the nature of his condition to a thing or the other. Without being able to rekindle the momentum to do exploit or to be a masterminded of the activities that lead one ahead. One might be a victim of complaining forever without having any reasonable curative measure to his disadvantages when care is not taken.

A normal human being is always accepting the irregularities around his destiny and get into the action to create betterment with all it takes to be made. Without the acceptance of the faults around one's destiny, there might never be acceptance of being liable and responsible for the solution around the issues.

The moment one looks into the matters around his destiny being caused by someone other than self turns him to be a slave to the condition. If you need to move ahead to attain purpose, there must be responsibility and there must be acceptance of the end result of all actions that are noted in one's life.

There is no kind of poverty that is not curable when there is determination to have them under one's control. If that is the case, it means that each of us must be able to realize our essentiality towards having a completeness of the nature and structure that can exterminate the hardship when they are encountered or experienced.

CHAPTER (THREE)

<u>CAUSES OF THE POVERTY</u>

There are numerous causes that can be examined. Some of the causes will be deliberated upon as we proceed.

- **Laziness**- one of the causes of poverty is an act of showing lackadaisical attitude to the issues of life. A man with the attitude of laziness might never be able to champion his life. Laziness is an act of being not comfortable to carry out job function or react to the issues of life as if they can be resolved. It has to do with the willingness and eagerness to cause a change or convert the situation around one to his benefit. A lazy man does not and might never see the need to be a master of destiny, but will always prefer to see the destiny or situation around him as being aligned with what God has for him. They tend not to see beyond the immediate circumstance, but see themselves as a slave to the situation rather than being continuously in charge till they are in possession of their destiny. They prefer living a comfortable life without having one. Most of their time is spent on relaxation nature of the activities other than being constructive and being involved in the selected circumstances that can translate their future to a better one. They are always not finding it easy to attempt the set of the activities that should remold them forcefully to regain their foresight. To say laziness, one can simply reason of the laziness of thought also. When one can not reason in-depth, it is termed to be laziness. There is none of the activities that can come into manifestation without being thoroughly thought off or considered. There must continuous thought and reasoning to make a turn around every time if one indeed in willing to experience the nature of change and life that is worth while to be involved with. They tend to attribute faults to everyone around them and those who have not assisted them while they grow. In nut shell, laziness is one of the most destructive elements to increase, and as a result of this, when it surfaces, it aggravates the intensiveness of the poverty.

- **Attitude to the situation**- the attitude or consideration to the issue one passes through really matter at the point of measuring the intense of the poverty. One can live in the poverty and at the same time he is not being influenced by the power of the poverty. Though he lives in the abject poverty, but he is control of the activities around him which makes him to think above the immediate circumstance to have different planning that can lead him out of the menace of the poverty. The attitude to the situation one goes through has a lot to say about the level of his poverty. Having physical cash does not mean that someone is not in poverty, but it only guarantees that he can meet up with his immediate desires. Any wealth or riches that does not look beyond the immediate need is confirmed such that can not overcome the power of poverty. Invariably, what this means is that, such individual is as well living in prospective poverty. Attitude is very relevant at the point of measuring the level of poverty. One might not have a dime in the pocket and yet, he is not poor because he can access different nature of the materialistic conditions that can end up the tensed situation around him. What a man can see and how he reacts to them have a long way to either reduce or aggravate the poverty level. Therefore, attitude to the situation around one is very expedient at the point of looking at the causes of poverty. A right attitude might never be involved in the poverty nature of living.

- **Illiteracy**- some one said that illiteracy is the greatest disease. This particular segment is in conformity with the statement. The ability to read and write is not connecting to being able to write or read formally all alone, but in connection with the ability to document your future and to follow it duely through the careful reading of the stages and attempts that makes it exhibit-able. There is need to be literate as regards the issue that should transform lives to better nature. What makes one not to be able to control the situation around him often leads to poverty. Being literate however makes one to be well understood of the tactics and the approaches in a systematic nature to assume authority or to have all it takes to construct a life that can never be subjected to poverty. Therefore, reading and writing of the situation and projecting on how best to have a definite solution is very relevant to be ahead of the poverty.

- **Blindfoldness or lack of exposure-** when you are not connected with the things around the world, you might not be able to understand what it means to act in a way or the other. What one can access is the basement for what he can conclude on or work on. Where you are matters at the point of taking decision in relation with the conversion of the odds to opportunities. Being exposed takes you round the world without moving an itch or moving around. It depends on the nature of reading or ideology you are clinched with. It has to do with the things that you shared or that you have considered with every other individual either good or bad while your conclusion is erected on your end result. It has to do with the listening to the information and being acquitted with the series of the activities that revolves around one. To then measure the poverty level, there must be consideration to the level of exposure and how cleared one is. Seeing beyond one's nose is quite very pertinent to be able to live above poverty. There must be full fine turning of mental configuration to attune to the ideology that should be created or make the necessary concepts that can lead a man ahead in all fields. Therefore, there is no way one will be blindfolded or not exposed and yet, he will live above the poverty level or have control over his destiny.

- **Adjustment to hardship**- one of the most killing agents of the living is the inability to resist hardship at the point of infliction. A nation or individual that adjusts to poverty or hardship automatically sets to visit its end. There are some things that one might never think to adjust to in life; one of them is poverty and hardship. These sets of destructive agents are meant to be well analyzed and resolved amicably other than adjusting to them. One of the major set back in the economy of most of the Africa countries is their inability to work out the solution to the problems around them, but keep adjusting. One of the major issues that we have been battling with from the time immemorial is the fluctuation in the rate of our currencies. I found it very rear to witness any of the currencies of the African nations devalued and after a time period correct itself.

Instead of the correction, what most of the nation do is adjustment. What I am saying is that, the causes should be more relevant than the adjustment. It is only a lazy minded nation that adjusts to hardship instead of finding a lasting solution to it. There should be solution to the prevailing problems when we are willing to have an outstanding outcome. Problems are made to be rectified. And sincerely, the nature of all problems we pass through from time to time should enlarge us mentally and make us to be able to think fundamentally to arrive at a conclusive end that should resolve the instability around us. Therefore, instead of the adjustment or maintenance, one should think of avoidance and curative measure to the issues around the world. When one is prone to the idea of adjusting to the issues around the world other than avoidance and looking for the curative measures, he is most likely to live in the poverty or hardship for a long time.

- **Lack of vision**- there must be vision before any form of any situation can be converted to one's advantage or benefit. Vision is quite very relevant at the point of taking crucial decision that can affect the situation around human nature. When there is no vision, race of life and projection are often run in an empty way or manner. A man without a vision is a man without a definite destination or structure that should lead him to his destination. It will never be fair not to know one's direction and bearing/ destination before one embarks on such journey. Any journey without a destination is a journey without a purpose. To live a purposeful life, there must definitely be a vision in accompany of such living. It is the vision that introduces you adequately to your intention and makes you to be in alignment with your end desire. To however be ahead of poverty, there must be a vision that is tantamount to moving over the poverty or the factors that can address the issues of poverty. One must be well affixed with a definite thing or the other that must be able to introduce your contribution to the world in holistic. The vision must be available to be able to do an appraisal of what you have done so far in line with your dream. A person without vision perishes suddenly without achieving anything meaningful. There must be a certain thing that must be a gazette to one's life to be able to function effectively to attain purpose. Vision is very expedient to be able to exterminate poverty or to live above it. Therefore, the nature of the vision that one has invariably measures if a man should live in the poverty or not. Hence, one can say that, lack of vision or substantial vision is one of the causes of poverty.

- **Inability to take decision**- when one does not have a vision, he might be afraid of taking decision that should affect him accordingly. There are some decisions that do not come ordinarily without having interest in them and your determination to take a step can help out. One must be able to tell himself at a point that this is what I want to do or these are the things I will not do. The courage to decide for oneself and to take a step to accomplish such reasoning is called decision. Decision has to do with those things that are done by you with the preparedness of accepting the glory or faults. Not minding what the end result can be, but with the expectation of the best always. To however live above poverty or ahead of poverty, there must be instance of taking decision and working in line with the decision taken. When decisions are not taken, poverty escalates.

- **Inability to be involved in the calculative risk**- there are certainly a lot of the nature of decision that are meant to be taken in life, but not all decision are lucrative and performing in nature. As a man, there is always the need to be assured of the end result of an action before they are taken. Decisions are taken based on the calculative risk. When you say calculative risk, you mean the kind of the risk that are being involved in as a result of the pre-information or certainty that they will definitely yield result, not an empty decision. One should be able to be calculative his decision to be involved in the decision that should create them or make them. Being calculative makes one to be predictive and more courageous to be involved. However, the level of poverty is rested on how calculative someone is in making attempts. To then move above poverty, there must be complete thought of being able to calculate effectively.

- **Destructive motive**- another very salient factor of the cause of the poverty is being inclined with the destructive motive other than constructive motives. A destructive minded man might never be able to look above the ordinary. A destructive minded might never be able to see the need to be involved in the activities which are in support of the existence that can create his destiny. He might not be able to think vigorously on what should be the contribution to the development of the world which invariably turns to be part of what makes him. When one could not see anything meaningful in the life of the others or in the things that exist or can not find a way to add up value to what he can see, then it means such a person is a replica of destructive motive. Destructive motive does not count the value or relevance of the information, idea or project before they are destroyed or demolished. If then the issue of destruction is in line with the values attributed to destructive minded, I am quite very indifference in their adverse effect on the poverty. The point remains that, at the point of destruction, one might not even know those things that are predominantly useful for him to be ahead of poverty. Hence, one of the major causes of the poverty can not be separated from the issues of being destructive in one's motive.

- **Lost of interest in the possibility**- there is no way one can be chained internally and yet he possesses control in the things around him. There is no way there will not be interest in what you do and you will be able to see clearly the benefits therein. There must be full interest in the things one gets involved with to be able to see the different possibilities that can emanate as a result of being involved in them. The issue of the interest as a cause of poverty can not but being well administered to know what it entails at the moment of correction. The kind of interest that one has on the situation and that which one has to overcome or control such situation is quite very relevant to make a thoughtful decision that can set one free indeed at the face of trial and hardship. Having interest in the possibility aspect of life makes one to realize that nothing is too difficult to be undertaken, it makes one to know that, the secret of success is in the ability to attempt it and to kick into action that brings forth the success of one's expectation. Even if one has found himself in a very ambiguous stage or state, he must realize that such a time does not last forever, and to be able to know what it entails to reason beyond the immediate circumstance to end the situation with good result. Having the interest in the possibility is what makes a man to live as if the situation around him is settled for the best. Therefore, to be a conqueror or a champion, having the mind set to have one on top of the situation around him is very expedient.

- **Inability to withstand rigor and training**- if one can not conclude within himself of the benefits that are in the rigors around him or the tensed situation he passes through, he might never count such time as moment of training and reformation in life. Yes, it is never a convenient time or kind experience to go through tough time, but within the experiences are enclosed bundles of advantages. There is no misfortune that is not fortunes creating when it is well processed. The secret of all the solution are rested on one problem or the other. Therefore, having challenges should be an avenue to increase at all cost, and this is the reason why one must never give up or think of the challenges, but to think of the varieties of the series of opportunities around whatever condition he has found himself. One of the factors that had made the poverty to persist can not be separated from the inability to count rigor and training therein as the bedrock to excellence when they are well treated and handled.

- **Too much of depending on the governance**- when there is too much of dependency on the government, the level of poverty get more tensed and aggravated. It is the responsibility of the government to make provision of some certain basic amenities for the citizens, but it might not be their right to force the individuals or populace into the making use of their dexterity and initiative to cause influence in the world. Most of the people attribute their inadequacies to the poor governance and inability to be assisted on a certain project or the other. I have not said, being assisted is not too necessary, but in its absinthial, other things must be done. What I am saying is that, having the full concentration on the government for what they need to do but they are not doing might be a cause for the inability to acquire anything in life. There must be urge to ordinary move ahead without having any issue being a constraint on your way or path to attainment. When one is reliance on the government for everything, he is depending on the government to take care of everything that has to do with the provision for his objective, sincerely speaking, government has more than enough things to get through with, which means that, it is very possible one's desire as regards the government intervention might not be possible eventually. One of the major causes of the poverty is over dependability on the government for their support and provisions which have really made more than enough brains to be wasted. However, there is always the need to be well enlightened and educated on the issue of being relent on the government to be able to move ahead accordingly and to achieve purpose in life. The fact remains that, a lot of the greatest achievers were unable to receive any support from the government, and they were able to come forth with something mystery, then why should we wait for the government till we can not achieve anything meaningful in life before starting something different? When mind is too centered on the government, it leads to poverty, because to be frank, no one can plan one's life for him if not by himself. Therefore, no one should be restricted or refrained from being active to perform accordingly rather than waiting for the government's assistance. If the government aids and grants come therein while you are already started your ambition, it can always be a plus to it. Controlling the poverty must have to do with the education on the government reliance to achieve cogent and important motive.

- **Inability to take full control**- in my book take charge, I have series of the information that were narrated and enumerated. I will like you to have your copy! Without being able to have the full control of your life or to be in control of what are in correlation with your destiny, one might never be able to access the greater height over the poverty or ahead of the poverty. Taking full control means, knowing that you are responsible for all what can happen or should happen as a result of your decision. All forms of flimsy excuses are excluded in your act or decision or aftermath result of your intention. Taking full control tells you that you are in charge not any other individual. It gives you the right of order to be ahead of the situation that might confront you. It means being the manager of the situation around your destiny and not allowing the foreign forces to take over. To live above poverty or to be a champion in life, there must be willing act to have control all over the conditions around your destiny. This makes you to be in charge, other than being a wagon; this however apportioned the rules that govern your life ordinarily other than by the other individuals or agents.

- **Choice**- one choice as regards his poverty level really matters at the point of evaluating it. Choice can never be counted out at the point of looking into the causes of the poverty. Sincerely, life is all about choice, and each individual has their respective choices to be taken at when due when they are being confronted either in a way or the other. The type of the choice you are involved in really matters when one is looking at the nature of the circumstances around him. What you could see matters to what you become in life. When all what you can see is impossibilities and comfort in the poverty, believing that someone will definitely come around to wipe it off for you, then you are yet to be prepared for the race to cross over. Crossing over requires being set to be crossed over, and it is all about the nature of the choice you have in you. If your choice is to live a wretched life, then your choice to move ahead of the poverty might not be effective or materialistic. If your choice is begging from a pillar to a post, it might be cumbersome for you to understand what taking over your destiny means. The nature of choice one has depicts the outcome of his purpose. To be rightfully connected with one's destiny and to be able to see distinctively, the nature of the choices around human existence matters.

- **State of mind**- what is state of mind? This can be the kind of the mind one has at the moment of receiving and accepting information.

State of mind is the condition of the mind in relationship to the immediate issue. It can be interpreted as the way at which certain information is accepted and processed to make a definite conclusion or end result. There are a lot of factors that are very critical to the instance of the state of mind. When one is provoked or offended by someone, his response to a certain issue or the other might be a bit influenced by the aggressiveness if he is not in control of his emotion. When someone has a certain thing or the other he is thinking of, such as heart broken, disappointment, loss, lack of a particular thing or the other, e.t.c, there might be influence of the effects of such things on his state of mind if care is not taken. Some set of individuals are very subjected to the influences on what happen to them which constitute their inability or incapacity to function as expected. What happened to some set of individual while they were still young or at their youthful stage and age still disturb them and they are as fresh as if they just happened to them. What you harbor in your heart really matters at the point of looking into the state of mind. State of mind has to do with your level of accommodating series of issues, either in respect of your benefit or disadvantage. I once had an encounter with a man, a driver that was taking me from a part of Abuja to another, he said that if he has the opportunity of being assisted with 500,000 Naira he will never be able to drive as soon as the information gets to him. I have also experienced many that were killed as a result of the celebration on what was apportioned without their expectation. What I am saying is this, anything can happen along the line of handling a certain transaction and information or the other, but they are not meant to be the justification to be shut of thought. The mind set and the nature of what you think at each time might be very valuable to be able to evaluate your level of performance and being able to overcome the poverty indices. The might set must be very active to command and instruct the internal factors to be well learned on what should be the right justification for a purpose, in which the issue of the poverty is not exempted.

- **Lack of innovation or emptiness-** there can never be any man in an empty state and yet, he looks at being ahead of poverty. One of the most critical natures of the causes of poverty is being at the state of lack of innovation and emptiness. When there is no clue or tactics to handle the issues of life, they become very cumbersome and difficult to be administered and offer a solution. Innovation makes something that has been in existence to be done as if they have never been done before hand. It brings the results that are fashionable and present to the issues at hand. Innovative ideas are responsible for the immediate situation without reference to how it was achieved in the years past. The solution can come in a similar way, but the ideology and strategy must never be similar. When innovation comes in, they travel far to affect the entire world in a way or the other. Innovation is an act of being creative to invent and to make provisions for the basic need and requirements of existence to ease their formal way of doing a certain thing or to start up with something that has unique direct or indirect effects on the nature of the activities around. Being empty means that one could not see anything worthwhile to create future. It means the inability to determine what are yet to happen with what is happening. It means having no access to the greatest advantage in the midst of disadvantages. It means the inability to see distinctively of the factors that should escalate the series of the processing that should be catalyst to the erection of the world class structure of the nature of living. To then discuss on the causes of poverty in holistic, there must be the need to relate on the series of the important features mentioned. There can never be a way out of the poverty if the individual is empty or have no innovative ideas or attitude. Therefore, to be ahead of the emptiness and undue pressure of poverty, there must be passion for innovation and all emptiness must be sealed off.

- **Inadequate acumen to integrate-** having full ideas of what are relevant to the world or that can be measure to the growth and development of the world is very essential, but the ability to integrate accordingly matters most. There are a lot of the ideas and issues around that were discovered, even at the point of reading through this text, very possible you have caught up with a certain thing or the other. The point remains that, without being able to determine the actual place of importance of your conceivable ideas, there might never be any genuine value that can be added to the world or to your development. Being able to determine the essence of a certain thing might not simply means, having the ability or the tactics that it entails to have them accomplished. When the strategies and values are not experimental in nature, they often turn to be no value eventually. It is quite very good to see a certain thing or the other, but being able to key in accordingly and to demonstrate the actual intention can never be overemphasized. To however be ahead of the poverty or to rule over the hardship around one's destiny, there is a must to be possessive of the qualities that can make the foresight to rule over the situation around and to be catalyst to the invention and demonstration of such values. Being able to integrate is however very essential to be able to have years of fruitfulness and converting the whole ideas of time being to an effective information and acts.

- **Procrastination**- as it is said, procrastination is the theft of time and a major constraint to attaining glory. There is no form of agenda that can not be attained. But there can never be any completion of any assignment without starting it. It is good to have vision and to have the various gazette to accomplish them either one after the other or collectively. But when the visions are not made to be manifested, then, there should not have been any need to converge on such vision. When what one supposed to do now is subjected to the future anticipated action or to be carried out in the time to come, it is said to be procrastination. Being unable to give meaning to the ratification of an issue when due or being able to act accordingly to resolve an issue or to do an act which can be done at the moment of consideration is called procrastination. Take for an example, one is meant to read each book in each day according to the time table set by him, but at the point at which a particular one should be read, he considered reading it in the following day.

Ordinarily, the structure or the time table is already impaired in the sense that, the book that should be read in the following day might not be read if care is not too taken. When one procrastinates, he wastes time. What this means is that, the time wasted can never be regained. Any time that is not well utilized is such that is gone forever. One of the irrecoverable and irretrievable resources is time. As soon as it goes, it goes forever without been able to recall it. When what is meant to be done is left undone, it turns out to be past tense and such time wasted can not be recall or renewed for it use again. Therefore, one of the causes of the poverty can not but be attributed to the procrastination of human in being engaged with an issue or the other without being able to fulfill the target. To be ahead of the poverty, there must be serious mind that is well determined to carry out operations when due and to be well involved in the activities that translate to the fulfillment of purpose at when due. Time management must be well counted reasonable to be managed to be effective and to deliver a situation above hardship.

- **Lack of the ability to yield to correction**- some set of individuals are extraordinarily good and sound, but they are often finding it difficult to yield to correction. There are some times that what one can see might not be well seen, therefore, if any one mention a certain corrective measure or the other that can be beneficial, they must be well noted and considered to be part of the success of such vision. Yielding to the correction in another trait that must be well learned to have the due progression and to be able to access the wealth of the information and techniques that can create a better standard of operational value that should make formidable activities that should create a better nature of outcome. There is no master of knowledge, and there can not be one. Learning is a key thing in life, and must be path way to success of everyone to adequately discharge responsibility. To be a learning minded person, it means that one is always willing to extract out the very best in the midst of the absurdity. It means the tender nature of the human that makes them to count the relevance in the life of the others. It means being able to pick up useful information from both the known and unknown to create a life of fortunes. It means the ability to access the information irrespective of their sources, sieve them and convert them to the greatest advantages that can be quite very useful to make a significant worth in the life of the extractor. However, the argument is that, one must be very adjustable to the correction irrespective of his status and qualification, because the race of life is quite very dissimilar to the issue of status and qualifications. What I am saying is that, if at all one is the best qualified in life in term of certificates and whole lots of qualifications, it does not really mean that someone of lesser qualification can not point out a suggestion which might be other than the kind of the qualification you have. Also, there are numerous things that when they are appropriately channeled, they will definitely yield result. If one is found in such a scenario, and someone tries to point it out, better to take to the advice to be able to make an edge way to provide the expected result. Also, when you are embarked on a certain project or the other, and there is an issue to be resolved, the correction should not be an ambiguous part of one's character. To be ahead of the poverty and to be able to create better future, there is extreme requirement of being yielding to the correction around the activities of the human beings.

- **Inability to learn**- learning is a key thing to the world development. It is very imperative to be learning principle minded to be connected adequately. When one does not have the attribute of learning, it amounts to the poverty in quote. To be able to see beyond ordinary, and to be able to do things that are mystery in nature, learning is very key. Having the nature of state of mind and composition that harbors information is very necessary to have a full grown self. To learn means to have the full passion for new ideas and to be willing to receive information that are not known by you. It is an act of sharing the notion of the others, while the benefits in the ideology are of more concern and of interest to the receiver. There is no situation that can be shifted or turn around without adequate information and exposure through learning. When one is unyielding to learning, he is been defrauded of more of his usefulness and importance. There must be a well adequate connection between what one does and what he learns to be able to have a better performance and difference. Therefore, learning habit can not be separated from the key attributes to the escape from the poverty or hardship of all natures.

- **Lack of strategy**-when strategy is excluded in the act of moving ahead in live, the whole situation turn to be tragedy. There are thousands of individuals that are well loaded in term of skill and ideas, but yet they can not achieve anything cogent in life. It is not about what you know or where you have been to sometimes, but by how best the very little you have can be strategically applied. There must be a specific tactic and strategy to accomplish any task if indeed the desire is to have such task attained. However, being strategically inclined means that, one is well processed and adequately planned to discharge a particular obligation in such a way to attain its success. Strategic individuals are not wasters of resources because they often try to get adequate information and dexterity to handle whatever they venture into in a successful manner. They are very diplomatic and sensitive to the issues around their intention, while they plan ahead to have a relative solution in case of unforeseen circumstances. They are of the mind with different nature of solutions to a single issue and they often know how best the human capital can be put into the full usage to accomplish a task. To however live above the issues that are surrounding the world, there is enormous requirement for being strategically made and to be systematic in all forms of approaches that can make up the intention. One of the most critical issues that must be well managed before crossing over the hardship and poverty must definitely be being strategically oriented.

- **Inability to consider ahead**- one of the natural constitute of the poverty in the Africa countries is the inability to think of the others. When one can only see himself or can only reason on his personal needs without being able to think further to see how others can be affected, it tends to create poverty. Most of the leaders and the followers are always of the chief thought of themselves, which has really negated the societal balancing. There is no way an individual, leader or followers can see himself and yet have a meaningful result on any aspect of his concern. Many leaders have turned to tyrant as a result of not being able to consider others, while many followers have been involved in the nature of the commitment that had aggravated the pains around them than being a solution. What I am saying is that, not being able to see others first in commitment might be one of the chief constitute of poverty. What brings expansion and development can never be separated from the attribute of being considerate of the others. A man can never be set to eradicate pains, and yet, he is self centered. There are some things that are handled collectively to have a lasting solutions, such is the issue of eradicating of poverty. What brings about the adequate adjustment and nullification of a situation of pains and hardship in the society can never be excluded from the ability to consider others first. Without being able to see others, the battle might change to self concern or purpose. To be absolutely out of the poverty therefore, being considerate of the others is very vital.

- **Lack of resource control**- to move ahead of poverty, there is need to be a resource control personnel. There might never be any substantial remedy to the issues of the pains and hardship if one is not resource manager. To be a resource manager means that one controls the resources and guides them from wastages. Spending lavishly and without understanding the tricks of spending might be termed to be waste of resources. Wasting of all nature of resources in one way or the other is termed resource wastage. There might never be any meaningful growth and development in the life of the individual, corporate body or government that does not understand the term resources control and work towards its full implementation. Having the resource control strategy in place, makes the extra ordinary things to be accomplished in an ordinary way. It gives the avenue and advantage to be strengthened enough during the implementation of a certain objective or aim. It gives the advantage of being able to expand as a result of the reserved resources, to create other opportunities other than the immediate opportunities. Resource control is however very pertinent to be able to cross over the issues of hardship and to be ahead of poverty. Without the management skill to have the full control over the resources, vision and undertakings are wasted.

- **Inability to take calculative risk-** there is no doubt that if one can not be able to take calculative risk he might not be made. Being calculative is being conscious of the aftermath effect of an action. It is an act of seeing or looking into the possibility around an action or attempt. It is a situation whereby action is not taken emptily or without cross examining its possibility. It is a state of being reasoned beyond the benefits of an action to know the best of the circumstances that might be resulted or be the outcome of such action. It is a state of being fully in connection of the end result of the assignment or involvement before being part of it. It is termed to be reckoning or estimation that depicts the outright information of what an end result of an activity should produce. There is always the need to be calculative at the point of embarking on any project or undertaken to be able to prevent waste. It is possible for a man that is worth billions of dollars to be wasted within twinkling of an eye if he is not calculative in his decision and attempt to move ahead. Also, it is very possible for him to double his investment or worth by being very calculative. Someone that is helped or generated resource by himself for living might be returned back to zero level if not into the debt if he is not well calculative. The argument is that, one of the most pathetic situations that determine the level of poverty is based on the ability to be calculative or not. When one is not calculative, he moves in depth into the abject poverty, and turn to a resource waster. To then, be ahead of the poverty, there is extreme need to be sensitive and conscious of the failure and the hazard in the projected job or obligation.

- **Fluctuation in the economy**- I just discussed on the issue of being calculative. Here, this illustration is centered on the set of the individuals that are not calculative. When there is fluctuation in the economy, there is every tendency of the populace falling victim of the instability. To have as an illustration, there were many individuals that felt victim of the fluctuation in the capital market in the years past. Many individuals believe that, no circumstance can cause the drop or devaluation in the stock market, but got to know that reverse was the case lately. The fluctuation in the economy or the price in the economy can be a source of poverty when people are not well educated on how they invest for the future benefit. Thousands of the members of the society have been translated to poor men as a result of their inability to understand what it means to be calculative in the aspect of the investment concern. In other way round, some people were found of keeping money in the bank for the future use, without knowing that, any money that is not effective and operational during the instability might never be able to withstand the instability in the economy. When there is fluctuation in the economy, the set of the individuals that are not financially educated are victims of the instability or adjustment as result of their novice and inadequate knowledge to understand the trick to deal with such fluctuation. There was a time at which the foreign currencies were extremely high, that is, there was devaluation in the currency (NAIRA). Many individuals went to purchase foreign currencies with the hope of selling them off when it gets to the peak, forgetting that there can be adjustment in the context of the Naira. It takes a man that trades with currencies to maximize his profit because the profit he would have made if at all there is fall in the foreign currency thereafter would be sufficient to maintain the sudden loss on the revaluation of such currencies that might surface unexpectedly. Except being too lucky, the repercussion of the fluctuation in investing into the currency or buying currency for the future benefit might be devastating. Many people were brought to the low level at the point of trying to take the risk which was never calculative. The major concern of the particular sub topic is to discuss extensively on the major issue that erupt as a result of the instability in the economy. There might never be any way poverty can be averted or prevented without having a very clever economy that does not fluctuate easily. However, one of the most deadly factors to the issue of poverty can not but being explained on the platform of the fluctuation in the economy of a nation.

- **Bad leadership**- it is now a very cleared and transparent issue that most of the countries have no issues other than their leaders that can not reason beyond what they can conceive. There is a very great issue for someone that can not see beyond his nose to be elected as leader. Leading entails the possibility of creating ideas and conclusion that are quite unbeatable for the onward increment in the situation around. To have what it entails to be well positioned economically, academically, logically and on infrastructures, qualitative leaders are quite expedient and relevant to create a radical positive impact. However, most of the leaders are not worth to be called one as a result of their contribution and ideological reasoning. There must be future which can be access and clearly noted in the mind of whosoever that should be a leader before being made one to see the expected end or outcome. The nature of the environment created by the act and reasoning of the leader however is very critical to be studied and to be cross examined to be able to have a cleared economic outcome and a befitting structure that can be hygienic for the perfect state of living. Therefore, having a bad leader automatically leads to the poverty and hardship, which means that, the nature of the leadership can easily depicts the nature of the situation in the world economy, and to measure the kind of the circumstance that one or collective individuals can find themselves within.

- **Bad electioneering**- just examined is the bad leader, but the process of electing them is quite very essential. Most of the political leaders did not elect themselves. They were elected by the populace. If that is the case, most of the leaders were chosen by us without verifying their past records. The most annoying aspect of it is that, most of the leaders that have disappointed us in one way or the other are often re elected due to their persuasive strategies with the money stolen from our purse. One of the most critical issues to be examined is the issue of picking up leaders, that had being one of the most active aspect of bone of contention to the poverty and hardship. I can not imagine someone without a good pedigree claiming to have the right sense of leadership. Most of the poverty is caused by the populace at the point of electing their leaders. When a wrong leader assumes duty, things get more deteriorated and the hardship waxes more stronger. There is always the essentiality of all the population having their right adequately represented by being well registered to perform their civic responsibility by voting and be voted for and to ensure that they vote for the right sets of the individuals and at the same time be committed when they are chosen. The cause of the poverty and hardship can not be well examined without being adequately looking into the immediate topic, while a due attention is given to it to produce better, and quantitative and qualitative leaders that can reason in a normal standard to affect the economy greatly and positively.

- **Lack of long term agenda and assessment**- I have been hearing of the different categories of the visions of all sorts, but only few of these vision work. There is a usual saying that where there is no vision, people perish, but when there is vision and the vision are not effective, people live in ignorance of no destiny. There might never be any reason to have a vision that does not work. Vision set that does not work is of the same value with the vision that is not set or seen. Most of the vision in the developing nations are often very super but they are never accomplished or attained as a result of the inability to do the needful assessment when due and to have continuity when there is change of political power. To be mind set to have a sustainable economy and to move ahead of the poverty, there is utmost need to have a rational vision, and to be able to carry out the vision thoroughly with a distinctive supervision and assessment while the continuity is not excluded. Most of the projects that should have added to our living standard are made to be wasted in nature. After huge amount of capital and fund had been committed to these projects, they are eventually abandoned, which thereafter turn to the mismanagement and waste of resources. Any economy that operates under the mismanagement and waste of resources will definitely be restricted in term of development and affecting the populace rightfully. Therefore, one of the major causes of the poverty can never but being unable to have a long term projects and assessment of their processing and continuity.

- **Over reliance on the certificate and qualifications**- the essence of the certificate must be well understood at the earlier stage of getting people to be enlightened. Being enlightened should be an embodiment of being well noted for the factors that can create a new life even where there is none. The issue of the certificate is quite very expedient but must be well understood properly before the younger generation ventures into it. Having a qualification that can not be well interpreted or allocated for its use is having a talent or skill that is not functional. There must be due conviction to what a man has to be able to allure its significant into the full uses. Many people have been to the school to obtain certificate just for its acquisition purpose, without being able to identify what the use of the qualification deserve. Turning certificate to smaller God that can give the very best of its nature without its due application can be a hindrance to having full control of the possibilities in the world. Certificates are meant to be an evidence of being certified for a certain job or to carry out an obligation, not to have it as the dictator of one's life. The whole essence of the certificate should be centralized on the mission to have a notable existence of its products. Being a certificated individual should be an avenue to be well exposed to the whole lots of the information that can be expedient to the dynastic nature of human behavioral pattern. However, to lead or to take the full possession of the destiny, certificate should be noted for its qualitative information that should be able to make hyper functional human beings. When human nature is centralized on the acquisition of certificate without imagining the whole essence of the real intention of being carrier of the certificate, they tend to relent on it or them, which means when there is no adequate provision or opportunity, someone that is with qualification might not be able to think ahead. The essence of the qualification and certificate should be rested on being liberated with the knowledge acquired rather than being a slave to the knowledge. When things are turned down, the whole essence of the academics acquisition should be the regulatory authority to make a conversion that should serve as the corrective measure. Therefore, when the reliance on the certificate is vast or enormous, the aftermath result of it effects often turn to deficiency in the independent nature of logics and thereafter become the contributor to the hardship and poverty.

- **Dependence on the white collar jobs**- this particular point is very common and often repeated most especially in the courses such as economics, commerce and other social sciences courses to be a contributor to the economic instability and regression. To live above the instability and economic issues, there must be priority to live not on the white collar jobs. Each individual are very essential at the moment of ascending to the apex of economic viability and stability, but when they fail to inject their contribution to the development, the impact becomes negation or stagnation in the economy. It is so sweet and palatable to be involved in the available jobs around, but there must be the sets of the individuals that are certified and segregated for the function of economic expansion and autonomy. Without the contribution of the populace to the defects and irregularities of the economy in term of various economic functions and activities, it might be too difficult for such a nation or economy to be liberated or collectively experienced full grown stage of performance. Just as discussed before hand on the issue of certificate and qualification, when the qualification and certificate are turned to the major tools other than being an influence of the disposition and technicality in men, the next option is to opt for the seeking of white collar jobs which has tremendously affected most of the African countries development and sustainability. Being too dependence on the white collar jobs as it has termed from the time immemorial has nothing a such to contribute to the economic viability but often turn people to the set of the individuals that are always relenting on the salary or wages other than being creative and innovational. Therefore, there is no way the factors that are responsible for the hardship and poverty can be treated in isolation in the absinthial of the dependence on the white collar jobs.

- **Application of the foreign extracted theories in the economy**- we often forget that what is obtainable in a country **A** might never surface in the country **B**. There are series of the propounded theories well tested in the various nations or economy which were adopted for the national use that had made the level of hardship and tense situation more complicated. The issues and the activities that exist around human jurisdiction must be very relevant to the nature of the propounded theory to confront them. When theories and gazettes of the other countries or economy are made to be the resolution or the remedy to another economy issues, they tend to add up additional unforeseen issues. The factors that are responsible for the theories around the world to be effective from a place to another are quite very different to themselves. The culture, race, religion, exposure, belief, availability of the resources, human power, strategy, e.t.c can never be over emphasized. Therefore, it is very relevant to be very vast in reading and to understand that all forms of all kind of the issues can be resolved and to form the basis of how it worked in the other economy, but never to form the impression of having such solution working in one's immediate economy or environment. My argument here is that, when the theory extracted from the other economy or world is straightly implemented in another economy, it turns to distortion and another set of issues which will definitely count the economy to be on the match time or stagnant nature. To however avert poverty or to control hardship, there is always the need to be operative in term of being able to study the relative issues around and to find a lasting solution to them. Imitating other economy is like invoking the additional issues to the already existing nature of the economy issues.

- **Over dependence on the others for assistance**- there might never be any way out of any issue if there is no self courage to resolve the issues. Counting on the others to be the sources of assistance might be an avenue to continue in the abject poverty and hardship. There is nothing wrong in accepting the offer for assistance or help, but it might be very irresponsible of anyone to count any one for the remedy of his predicament. Issues are meant to erupt, and they are coming forth just because they are needed to be found the lasting solution to them. There are many series of the issues that come forth from time to time, which when one reasons critically on them, they can be resolved. Most of us tend to rely on the other individuals to have solution to the issues. To be frank, any issue that one does not determine to resolve might live forever with such an individual. Relenting on the others to resolve issues is always very devastating issues that might not make the issues to be resolved if care in not taken. However, being over dependent on the other is one of the most critical stage or factors that bring about poverty and hardship. Poverty and hardship detest someone believing in himself or having the courage to take a move to make an end to it. To then think on the factors that bring about poverty, there must be a reason to consider not being over dependence on the others to have a solutions.

- **Use of the outdated philosophy and tactics**- just same way the idea of the foreign extracted nature of the theories are not the best options to the economic efficiency and improvement to control poverty level, the use of the outdated philosophy and tactics might be very deadly to any economy that wants to grow. The set of the established theories in various professional bodies are re-modified and upgraded from time to time, so also is the need for the philosophy and logics to the development. Operating on the outdated logics and philosophy is like consuming the outdated drugs. What is meant to resolve issues tend to aggravate it, which as a result of this leads to another phase of torment and inconveniences. If the issues to be resolved or to be rectified are enclosed within the nature of the kind of the abnormality in the human environment which is happening or guiding against its occurrence in the nearest future, then what this means is that, the nature of the approach to be given must be alive and current. However, to have an overview of how poverty is involved in the discussion, there is always the need to have a living and current solution to the prevailing issues if one desires to be exonerated from the deficiencies of the poverty.

- **Reasoning without implementation**- to move out of poverty, there is always the need to be reasoning minded, but not only a reasoned, but being able to implement the reasoning. There is no reasoning that is not effected that can be useful for the use of reducing poverty. There must be a working reasoning and logics to be out of the hardship. When one desires to resolve issues and yet he does not get to the stage of its experimentation, it becomes a waste and inactive. To be in control of the destiny, there must be the need to control plans and reasoning. There is no plan that is not demonstrable that can be effective for the essentiality of making difference, most especially in relation to the issue of hardship or poverty. To control poverty, there must be functional implementation of reasoning and logics.

- **Unavailability of social amenities and infrastructure**- the essence of the government is to create the social amenities and infrastructures for the use of the citizens. When the government is very in perfect state as regards making provisions for the social amenities and infrastructures, the citizens enjoy the benefits of being benefactor to the provisions. There are many of the provisions that are very essential to the wellness of the economic viability, while the issue of preventing poverty can not be exempted from it. Many of the numerous good ideas and intention are dying just because there is no light or electrification in the developing nation and undeveloped economy.

Some of the productive activities are solely relenting on water supply. In case of no water supply such activities are impaired. Another worthwhile provision that is very demanding for the competency and efficiency of the citizens or to explore their inbuilt skill and talent effectively is road. Good road is worth to be mentioned at the point of moving ahead of the poverty. So also there are many others amenities that are very necessary to be catered for to be able to move ahead of hardship or poverty, such electrification, schools, hospitals, e.t.c. Hence, availability of social amenities is very compulsory for the eradication of poverty.

- **Community unrest and war**- this is another measure of evaluating the hardship or poverty. There are series of the economy encompassing with the uproar and disunity. There might never be an avenue for the advancement and development in the economy that is filled with discord and war among the citizens. When there is community unrest or war, the economic function are restricted and impaired, this however make it very impossible for the atmosphere that can accommodate the due nature of the growth and development. There is no way there will not be harmony and peace and there will be advancement in the economy. Therefore, to move ahead of the poverty, there is always the need to be able to reason above disunity and the exuberant nature of the misunderstanding that prevent foresight and vision to be active and accomplished. During the unrest and uproar, it might be very difficult of the populace to be in control of the activities around them, and by so doing, there will not be room to tackle or go against the hardship or poverty. To have a complete living or life, there must be essential need to be in the midst of the conducive atmosphere where reasoning can be accessed, deep thought can be given and there can be full implementation of purpose.

- **Discontinuation in learning and lost of value for reading** - a man might never be able to see more than what he can see or think without being able to be learned in a continuous manner. There is no limit to the learning if actually one desires to have it. There are numerous sets of the information that if one has been in association with would have added value in a way or the other to one, but when they are not attended to when due, they are more strengthened and bigger than one's thought at the point they are meant to be applied. Learning entails both formal and informal kinds of education. It is very possible for each an individual to learn at least a trick or thing in a day. So, it is very demanding that, one should be engaged in the continuous learning to be able to relate at the pedestal that he should to be able to move over the hardship of all natures. So also, the habit of reading, the value is lost already in the society. There is always the need to have the passion and zeal for reading. A reader is a leader they use to say, so also, one can have the key to the huge of information around the world without moving an itch if he reads. A reader can never be a dullard or a novice of the appropriate standard to the relative issues of life. The more you read, the more you have the possession of the future and the things around you. Reading is the key to living a current life and fine turning destiny. However, if one desists or refuses to learn or to read, it becomes an issue that might be affixed with the issues that translates to the hardship and poverty. There might never be a way at which the causes of the poverty can be accessed, well analyzed and resolved without the full consideration of the being acquitted to learning or reading.

- **Restriction in thinking other than thinking of how to affect the world in holistic**- to be a fulfilled individual or entity, there must be love to affect the world without restriction in the kind of the individuals to be affected. There must be a structure that can carter for the entire world without being biased or being compromised with the inequalities in the world. To be able to affect the world, there must be a total connection with the entire nature of the individuals who are meant to feel the impact of your contribution. The more the numerical strength of those who a man can be extended to measures the strength of how viable the intention is in the world. Looking into the general aspect of life other than looking into the restricted areas is very necessary to make a huge contribution that might be noted and well celebrated from generation to the other. To then move ahead of the poverty or hardship, there is always the need to move in line with the operations that are centered on affecting the entire world. The bigger the area of encompass, the higher the value of your reasoning to affect the world. Therefore, thinking outside the box to formulate the hypothesis and nature of value that can cut across the world and that can affect the entire world is relevant at the point of looking into the nature of the desire and activities that should be proper for the enlargement and moving ahead of the hardship.

All these sets of the factors that were enumerated are just the part of the consideration of the causes of the hardship and poverty. To however be ahead of it, they must be corrected according. I will like to move ahead to the negative impart of the poverty and hardship.

CHAPTER (FOUR)

IMPACT OF POVERTY IN THE SOCIETY

There are many impacts of poverty in the society. There are numerous things that occur as a result of being in hardship or a state that is not desire by the individuals. The sets of the outcome that are visible in the society that lives in the poverty are thus follows;

- **Insecurity** – insecurity can be said to be the situation at which the society or an economy tend to find itself in the midst of one problem or the other that can be associated to the issue of general insecurity. When people find it very difficult to sleep with their two eyes closed, they live in an insecurity situation. When one can not travel to stay at which ever place of desire within or outside, it amounts to the insecurity. When there is tribal discord or religion crisis, this is an act of insecurity. These and other natures of the outcomes are very significant to the situation at which the society lives in the hardship or poverty.

- **Untimely death**- life span of the people is shortened as a result of living in the poverty or hardship. People tend to think of the irrelevant things instead of being composed and reformed to formulate the new tricks that are necessary for the assignment of the adjustment. People grow old fast without any reason. There will always be panic and tension which often translate to high blood pressure that makes a lot of the individual to die untimely. Some set of the individual think of no alternative to living **and** by so doing, they commit suicide and others atrocity. There is a saying that, the cowards die before their time. This is the exact instance of living in the poverty when one perhaps does not have the situation being under the control.

- **Lack of vision**- there is no way there can be vision or inspiration when there is no food in the stomach. I often write and get involved in other creative activities. There is no day that I will be left with nothing in my purse or pocket that I will be able to catch up with the right inspiration.

There are inspirations that are in lineage of your state of mind. If one lives in poverty or hardship, there might never be any form of the inspiration that will be encountered. When the state of mind is disordered, there might never be a genuine vision. Planning requires a perfect state of mind. There might not be vision in the midst of the poverty and hardship.

- **Lost of sight and passion**- just like vision; sight and passion are at the same time very relevant. Ability to see ahead or making some reasonable decision that can ameliorate the situation that one passes through is having a foresight. In the midst of an unsuitable situation, there might never be an avenue to be connected with the right foresight to forge ahead. Similarly, passion means the zeal to do things in an extra ordinary way. There might never be any passion or zeal to do what you delight to do when there is poverty or hardship around someone. Therefore, the situation that leads to poverty is a situation that bring about lost of sight and passion.

- **Criminality**- one of the most significant natures of the hardship and poverty is criminality. When there is poverty or hardship within the enclosure of the society, many tend to be engaged in the criminal acts and other illegal functionalities that can place a plate of food on the table for them.

- **Political instability**- political instability means not being able to have stability in the political power. It often amount to the inability of the head of the state to spend his tenure completely as a result of either pressure around him or killing him while in the office. It can as well be noticed on the nature of the intermittent discord of the populace and the incumbent power. This and other outcome are noted in the midst of poverty and hardship

- **Economic instability**- the issue of the economy is very necessary to have a full function and activities that can guarantee future. The issue of economy has to do with the kind of trade and industries within the nation, financial aspect of the nation, fiscal and monetary issues, e.t.c. All these sets of the consideration are relevant at the point of looking into the issues that got to do with the hardship in the society. To be frank, these sets of the analyzed factors are the ones in custody of a stable economy, and there is no way there can be an abnormality in any of them that poverty will not dominate such society. When they are not working effectively, it means the economy is not stable and it can only be in an unstable stage as a result of hardship and poverty. This is when people have nothing to contribute anymore or could not see the important of contributing to the society.

- **Embezzlement**- often at times we ask ourselves some salient questions on the cause of the mismanagement and embezzlement. There is no other cause than being living under the mental poverty. I will relate on the mental poverty in the next chapter. When one lives under the mental poverty, he lives as if everything should belong to him. However, any opportunity to convert the resources of the populace to his in any nature becomes a privilege or advantage. When someone is paid and yet he is stealing, it means there is something wrong with his level of thinking and associated mental functionality. Stealing public funds and resources is as a result of mental deficiency and poverty. Pathetically, the society now celebrates the thieves and rogues that are meant to be kept in the cell. Embezzlement is one of the major results of the poverty and hardship.

- **Killing and robbery**- I mentioned criminality before now, killing and robbery can as well be enlisted under the criminality. When poverty rules and hardship are visible, there is always unnecessary killing and shielding of blood and carrying out of attack on the other fellow human being just to have means to get one's livelihood. This act is generated as a result of hardship and poverty.

- **Waste of ideas and innovation**- ideas and innovation that are meant to be constructional factors for the way ahead or to move to the next level of the economy become wasted and not useful when the poverty and hardship are the other of the day. The citizen and the governance will never be able to see the need to have investment in the lives of those who are doing a thing or the other to influence the world or the economy. The condition at which the society operates will be the very best they can consider to operate without looking ahead for other relevant new version or way to accomplish development and growth. However, when the owner of the ideas and innovation discover that they are not meeting with their standard in term of their living condition or perhaps, the citizen do not have the interest in the nature of their effort to ameliorate the situation, they have no option than to move out of the track to either apply for white collar job or other obligation that can assist them on their living standard. Therefore, the nature of the ideas and innovation become waste and immaterial.

- **Dead end destiny**- when the ideas and innovation are not allowed to work as they should or encouraged to be displayed, it amounts to dead end destiny. No destiny can be created without being function in the line of the destiny. To have a destiny, there must be provision for the avenues to make it working. In a situation where there is no structure to encourage what you have the delight to do, one is forced out of his line of destiny to run after a different destiny which in never by willingness. This amounts to dashed of destiny and its wastage. To be a destiny carrier, there must be a destiny that one pursues. Without running after a certain destiny, there can never be achievement and attainment of such destiny. However, when destiny is abandoned by the owner of the destiny, they become unaccomplished in their kinds. This is however one of the major consequences of the poverty and hardship.

- **Inability to give maximum trial-** when the environment at which one lives is not conducive or appropriate enough, the number of attempts to complete an action becomes minute. The strength to be involved in the functionalities till they are reality becomes no where to be found. People tend to move away from various undertakings that should be an avenue for the betterment of their lives or future as a result of their failure in the first attempt and knowing that the effort might run into the dead end eventually. Poverty and hardship make the people to think of their stomach first before other things. However, continuous trial and effort to gain the full control of the future might be termed as wastage without minding the end result. So, the inability to give maximally is made up of the hardship and poverty.

- **Flimsy excuses**- this is one of the most detestable outcome of the hardship and poverty. People tend to forget that they are responsible for their lives. They often attribute faults to various things around them. Some of the excuses are looking into the bad governance to be the actual cause of their incumbent state. Pointing the accusing fingers to the brothers, uncle, parents, e.t.c to be the cause of their poverty. There is none that should be faulted for your fault to do the right thing that should lead you ahead in life. Giving of the flimsy excuses is just a measure to waste your time and to count yourself out of the needful success. A successful minded individual is never a complaining individual, but a determined individual to face the challenges of life. However, at the point of hardship and poverty, there is every tendency to give undue excuse other than being kicked into the action that should translate situation to a better one.

- **Wickedness**- wickedness takes place in different ways. It can be examine at the angle of being not fair to the other human beings. Planning of series of evils or things that can reduce them other than elevating them is termed wickedness. There are some actions that we often do not consider while looking into the act of wickedness. Some people believe that being cruel at the point of giving money or material things is just wickedness. Sincerely, it goes beyond that. Inability to give an advice that should create avenue for the betterment in quote in wickedness. Not being able to think to the level of affecting others in a certain way or the other is a sign of wickedness. Inability to have the kind likeness that should make you to know that you are worthwhile as a creature is wickedness. Having joy in the pandemonium of all sorts that affect humanity negatively is wickedness. Our wickedness is often well known to us, they are the ugly incidences or attitude towards humanity. However, the major cause of this is often responsible to the hardship and poverty nature.

- **Discord and uproar**- where the poverty and hardship rules, there is always the discord and unnecessary disagreement on the irrelevant circumstances or situations. Something happened sometimes in a neighborhood very closed to me. A graduate with distinction has been looking out for a job, but was unable to get one. Along the line, on a faithful day he went out as usual without no penny in his pocket, and at a time he needed water, thirsty. However, instead of begging for water he decided to pick up a chacet of water out of the bags kept outside a super market and the manager of the super market caught him during the action. However, the manager shouted thief while the wounded lions and frustrated touts came out with different ammunition to beat him and eventually set him ablazed. What I am saying is that, poverty is a great disease that does not allow straight thinking before kicking into the action. The cost of the charcet of water as at then was N5.00 which was quite very insignificant in worth compares with the judgment and death sentence. Also, transfer of aggression and dispute between the citizens is visible. Fighting on the insignificant circumstances and things is very constant in nature. These kinds of ugly incident can not be exempted from the negative outcome of the poverty and hardship.

- **Too much of concern to monetary and material things**- there is no doubt to conclude that one of the major result of the poverty is having too much of concern to monetary and material things. There is always too much of thinking haphazardly at the point of hardship. The effect bounces on the reasoning and logical contents of the human. They tend to think of the possibility of gaining world at the detriment of wasting other human values and lives. The concern for material and monetary close up the in-depth understanding of the populace to establish a system that can nurture a better standard of the time to come. However, poverty and hardship are constitute of having too much of the concern for the irrelevant things other than being constructive to make a conducive and exceptional society.

- **Lower education standard**- there is no way a society can be ahead of the other nations without being at the right state of full operations. An economy can never be balanced without being at the right session and level to have such expected result. Education is very key to the height at which the economy can attain. Education is the bedrock of the nature of the society that a nation inspires to have. Education is light and the glory to determine the destiny of any economy. It is said to be the avenue to climb to the height of honour and to decide on the path to the attainment of the projected envisaged intention. There is no economy that can survive without the full influence of the real educational sector that should make up the yardstick to the factors that control the technological and innovative world. In fact, education is the major element to the economic development and adjustment. Therefore, in case of any defect in the economy, it is as a result of the poor basis for the education. However, at the phase of the poverty and hardship, the tendency for the standard of education drops to the barest minimum as a result of looking for what to eat and other demands and requirement ahead of the need to have a standard education.

- **Lower technology**- the issue just discussed is lower in the standard of education. This aspect however relates on the consequence of the lower standard of the education. Saying education might not mean the formal aspect of the education all alone, but it contains both the formal and informal nature of the education or better to say, all acquired knowledge. Without being inclined with the knowledge that should connect one to the opportunity in the area of definition or concentration, there might never be the understanding of coming into the involvement of such incidents.

Technology has to do with the perspective of reasonability to ease the tension or the inconveniencies around the environment of the world. What a man sees has to do with what he can stay in connection with as regards what he can think of. And what you can think of is relative to what you are exposed to. To however have a thorough technological development and advancement, there is always the need to stay out of the poverty and hardship. When there is no food in the stomach or money in the pocket, there is always every tendency of not being in the right frame of heart to think vigorously to command the activities around the environment. However, the poverty nature of the economy or nation has a greater impact on the standard of the technology and innovation.

- **Insatiable desires**-poverty is a bad omen that makes the world and the people therein to be insatiable in their desires. What do I mean by insatiable desire? It means the act of not being able to get satisfied in term of wants and other relative requirements of life. It means the act of not being able to have a stated height of consumption or agenda before planning for the others around them. It means being not social and generous in the midst of plenteousness. It means a situation at which one could not think of the others in term of being a blessing to them. It can simply be identified as a condition at which there is severe urge for more of the consumption at the expense of their irrelevances. However, stage of insatiable desire is brought about by the reasoning of poverty and hardship. There is no way there can be hardship and the people will be satisfied. They will always have the urge for more at the expense of their limit because of the fear of the unknown and the uncertainty of tomorrow. Therefore, as part of the consequences of the poverty, insatiable desire can not be left out.

- **Worship of money and human beings**- there is always the case of worshiping of money and human beings when there is hardship and poverty. Many individuals find it difficult to reason vastly when they are in bondage of hardship; they tend to worship the material things. Material things and human being are turned to the smaller gods just to have survival and to be able to live ahead of the poverty. Therefore, the situation at which poverty and hardship control is subjected to the disposition of worshiping of money and ordinary beings.

- **Lost of being counted serious**- when there is poverty and hardship, there is always the lost of being counted serious as a result of the empty pocket or drain pocket. With the fact that you are not able to control your life or being able to handle the situations around you, the world counts you to be an incompetent personality. One is made not to be equated to his worth and what he carries. He is looked down on based on what they can access other than what he can do or demonstrate. No matter the logics and ideas are, they are considered inferior as a matter of his present nature or condition that is not permanent. Often he will be looked or assessed as someone who does not have anything meaningful to contribute, whereas, he has thousands of uncountable things to offer. This is one of the most dangerous consequential results of poverty.

- **Inability to meet the immediate desire**- this is one of the definition given ahead. Hardship and poverty make one to be handicapped in term of having access to the immediate desire and need. It means that one might not be able to pick up what he likes or desire to use immediately at the point of wants. Each individual has their needs and desires at a point in time, and when these desires are not met at the moment they are required, sometimes it becomes not relevant again. Take for an instance, a man desires to pick up a school entrance form for admission, but he could not get the expected money to doing so at when due till the expiration of the form. If peradventure, he was unable to get the money after the expiration of the form, this means that the intention is no longer valid for its purpose at the time of having the money. Therefore, to close the analysis up, being not able to meet up with the expected or immediate desires is one of the major causes of the poverty and hardship.

- **Discontinuity in development**- one of the most critical issues that emanate as result of the poverty and hardship is discontinuity in the development. People do not have sufficient financial strength to move ahead to complete their projects. On the other hand, in the aspect of the governance, they find it difficult to continue with the projects set aside, but rather, they tend to look out for the loop holes that can generate revenues into their personal pockets. If one is not assured of his tomorrow, he might not be able to see the world at the right perspective to do what he should do to affect the world accordingly, but rather, to be more of consideration on how to be able to accrue wealth injuriously or illicitly to meet his future needs. However, when what you can see are the unforeseen circumstances instead of the opportunity, there might not be any avenue to see the need to be fully inclusive in the aspect of the provisions that should add up values to the life in holistic, whereby the project can not be under stated.

- **Inability to think straight**- straight thinking requires a stable mind that can reason accordingly to have perfection. There is always the need to be a reasoning minded to be able to grow and to add meaningful contribution to the nature of the world. When one can not see rightly, he might not be able to get any thing rightly done. Accomplishments are based on the result of the things that can be seen within. If one does not see anything and he can not see anything, it simply means that, seeing what should stand as catalyst to his successful ending might never be attained. There is a need to constantly see something worthwhile to move ahead in life. However, to see something meaningful, there is essentiality to have the capacity to think rightly. It might be very difficult if not impossible for someone to be engaged in the thorough thinking without having a stable mind, and part of those things that must be considered to measure the level and status of the mind is poverty or hardship. Therefore, one of the major consequences of the poverty and hardship can not be separated from the inability to think straight.

- **Fear of unknown**- when one says fear of unknown; he means the nature of timidity and unnecessary panic without justification. He means the sensation of discomfort in the futuristic outcome of what nature has to offer or of what should happens either one injects value or not. It means the inability to have the conclusive thought that the situations are being controlled by the kind of the investment of the men in term of their economic activities. However, one will definitely be inflicted with the fear of unknown when the situations around one in not pleasant and tranquil. There is no doubt, to have the effrontery and ability to think above the fear of unknown; one must understand what it means to be able to live ahead of poverty or hardship.

- **Lack of tender mind to create opportunity for others**- there is a kind of inferiority complex and lack of courage to make out opportunity for the other in the midst of hardship and poverty. One becomes self centeredness other than being able to have the expansion in the holistic thought to create opportunities that should bring forth other opportunities. If we are looking at the remedy to the world issues, there is always the requirement of being involved in creating opportunity. Many have nothing to offer in the world and yet, they stand as the major constraints to the upcoming in term of their vision. If at all you must criticize any form of work, such criticism must be constructive to affect the logics around the development in a positive way. There must be interest in the creation of the avenues that can make others, while those ones that are availed the right of the order as well open up other opportunities. When there is no creation of the opportunities in the world, the world gradually returns back to desolation. The space is very large and quite wide to accommodate the whole nature of the desire of men. Industrialization and innovation must never be handled with levity at the point of moving into the stage of economic completeness and advancement. However, to be able to have such soften mind and tenderness kind of mind that can invent opportunities, there must be a nature of the environment that is adequate in term of being excluded from the poverty and hardship accordingly.

- **Ineffectiveness of governance**- the impact of the hardship and poverty are direct to the efficiency of the government. There are more individuals counting on the government when the economy is at the unimaginable barest minimum standard. Poverty makes the government contribution to the economy to be very weakened. When the populace can not be self reliance, it always centers to having maximal relent and concentration on the government. There are several kinds of the amenities and creation of jobs and opportunity that are quite very important to the citizen to be able to make the world of their advantages. Most of the citizens should be at the other end of the world but yet, they are yet to be reformed or constructed to make their real life. There are numerous thought and vision that are very necessary to the expansion of life, but when they are not utilized, they have no meaningful impact in the world. When people find it difficult to convert their inbuilt capacity to privilege, they become ineffective and useless to the society. Many talent and trait have been wasted due to the lack of the availability of the factors that should lead the vision out of their crude nature. Take for an illustration, many organization have been liquidated as a result of the unavailability of the electricity. Though they have a very outstanding vision and foresight, but they are liquidated with their effort on the kinds of the organization established. The sets of the individuals that are victim of this circumstance must as well live, which make them to be more dependable on the government. However, government has a lot of commitments to attain. When numerous individuals are depended on them, it becomes a serious issue that translates to ineffectiveness of the governance. This then stand as one of the challenges of the hardship and poverty.

- **Illiteracy**- when the stomach is empty and there is no cleared accessibility to the future, there is always the emerging of the illiteracy. Many people have the delight in being well learned and out-rightly educated, but they are cut shut of their dreams as a result of the nature of the environment they live in. In the hierarchy of needs, food, shelter and other factors must be in place before you can think of the other things. If these essential factors are not met, there might be cluelessness and inability to reason in a perfect order. Going through the kind of drilling that should create betterment and genuine difference becomes very difficult if not unattainable. Schools and vocational centers are abandoned for what should place food on their table. However, poverty and hardship are the sources of this nature of attributes.

- **Deny of destiny**- when one is unable to access the stages that should create him or he is unable to formulate the nature of the structure that should make him his real personality, it leads to deny of the destiny. Destiny that is not well planned or executed is a denied destiny at the long run. What makes destiny to work is lured with its efficacy to be demonstrated. However, with the series of the enlisted delinquencies, one can conclude that, if one is not advantaged to be in charge of his destiny or to have the full functionalities that should make out the destiny, such destiny can be denied. One of the major issues of the hardship and poverty can not be excluded from this point.

- **Greediness**- I have said a lot of things in respect of the greediness in the points above. If one can not be able to create opportunities for the others, he can not be able to think of the others first. He does the economic functions that the world can not benefit from, he can not assist other to attain their destiny, embezzles, e.t.c, these are all the signs of the greediness which are tantamount to the hardship or mental poverty. In the circumstance at which hardship and poverty dominates, there is always the element of greediness that make most of the people to count the other individuals to be no one, and as a result of this, they tend to look after being in the possession of the resources of the world. Though they have, but it can never be sufficient for them, and as a result of this, they remove the entire interest in the other people, and often think of their selfish interest. Greediness can never be counted out of the consequences of the poverty and hardship.

- **Lost of vision**- visions are perished and ineffective when there is hardship and poverty. To have vision means having plan and foresight to the attainment of a particular objective. Visions are however lost when there is no standard environment that can allow such vision to be in place. When on says destiny is denied, it means that there was no standard vision to attain the structured objective which could have taken him to a stage of no limitation. In the midst of the instability and hardship, vision becomes mere dreams without being able to attain them. It might be very disadvantaged of someone that can not organize vision to make out any substantial outcome at the course of economic injection of values and intention. However, having a strong vision has to do with being able to clearly define the intention and to have the in-depth understanding of what one desires and how to make such intention actualized. A good vision might never be emerged or emanate in the midst of hardship and poverty, that is to say that, if at all vision are connected with, it is very possible to found such vision wasted and unused as a result of the delinquencies of the hardship and poverty.

- **Inability to determine right from wrong**- the capacity to differentiate right from wrong is one of the key solutions to the world. When the right thought are conceived to be wrong or wrong is conceived to be right, there will definitely be challenge or challenges. There must be yardstick that must be vast enough to understand the kinds of decision and their effect on the world economy. I tend to ask myself some questions on the reason why most of the Africa countries are not yielding accordingly to the various ideologies that had be propounded. Actually, to evaluate the workability of theory, there is need to check into the different segments of the economy to check their responsiveness to such theories propounded. Many theories are ordinarily good and alright at the point of their initiation, but they might never be the best for the economy under discussion at the point of their recognition and application. One must be able to check the viability and reaction of the other sets of the factors of the economy to cross examine the appropriateness of the theory. However, being able to cross examine the theory to be right or wrong is very pertinent to be able to have a resounding result. On the other way round, to be able to know the right from the wrong as an individual, there must be a thorough examination of understanding of how to be involved in the activities around the world. When wrong tactic in keyed-in in a right environment, the outcome is wrong result. Also, when the right tactic is injected into the wrong environment, the answer becomes wrong feedback. There must always be the efficacy to dissect the outright worth and value of the decision to be applied to have a definite conclusive expected result, else, reverse will always be the case.

However, because of the inability to have the time or the attitude to be in control of the situation around one as a result of hardship or poverty, the instance of the inability to determine right from the wrong is vivid and apparent.

- **Juvenile delinquencies**- juvenile delinquencies is always formed to be part of the criminality that was mentioned ahead. It is an act of seeing the juvenile or the growing ones to be involved in the nature of the criminality in the economy. These sets of the activities can be mentioned to be caused as a result of the hardship and poverty, and they can be accessed through; being fraudsters, harlots, rituals, turgery, 419, cyber crime, robberies, kidnapping, e.t.c. These and other sets of the consequences are very related to the issue of the hardship and poverty. When the younger ones discover the mutiny and disruption, most of them that are not too courageous tend to wage into these sets of acts. Therefore, the inability to control hardship and poverty is the main causal factor of the sets of the activities enlisted.

There are others consequences that might not be reported or illustrated here, we shall be available to receive more from the audience, and there will definitely be an upgrade from time to time.

CHAPTER (FIVE)

<u>DISSIMILARITY BETWEEN THE MENTAL AND MATERIAL POVERTY</u>

As said before in one of my statement at the point of looking into the definition of the poverty, there are a lot of the factors that must be cross examined or cross checked to be able to reach a conclusive end of what poverty really means. Being in need of a certain thing or the other might not be referred to poverty.

As I said before now, in the definition given above, it is very possible to have nothing in your pocket and yet, someone has something upstairs. When you have what can take you out of poverty and you work toward having such a thing to translate your destiny accordingly or to stand as a catalyst to being advantaged to be at the highest pedestal, then you are not living in the poverty. Your ability to manage yourself and to look beyond the abnormality around your destiny counts you to be outstanding if you do not relent or take yourself to be a failure.

Most people were born in the abject poverty and many were even living it before they were conceived. As a matter of reality, this might not really have anything to do with the kind of the world or life one has in plan for himself. To be in poverty means the incapacitation to know that there can be remedy to the instance of poverty. Sincerely, it is better to be financially poor than being mentally poor.

The hazard of being mentally poor is constructional work to extend poverty to the generation to generations. It can also be said to be an instance whereby what one has or his skill and talent are not functional or active for the purpose of the advancement in the world economy or in the lives of the less privileged. Creation of the activities that can lead to other activities which can declare a better future is very relevant to conquer poverty; else, the inability turns poverty to a visible wrong instance in the context of economic assessment. When the right things are not touched or the right things are not implemented, it is an instance of poverty.

When what one conceives often is to seeing to the down casting or demotion of the others, it is a sign of poverty. Inability to contribute immensely to the recreation and restructuring of the economy and the advancement of the world is poverty, and so on as so forth.

However, a lot of definitions were given before now on both material and mental poverty, this particular segment is to differentiate on these sets of considerations.

Material poverty means the inability to eat three square meals per day. It means being not able to carter for the necessity of life like shelter, clothing, housing, transportation, payment of bills and rates, e.t.c. It means not being able to have access to free movement or accessibility. It can also be said to be the inability to access freshness in education. Material poverty has to often do with the visible or things that can be evaluated immediately.

It has to do with the present needs which are based on the yardstick that stands as a measure to evaluate its standard in term of accomplishment or their degree of immediate satisfaction.

Mental poverty however means mental deficiencies to do right thing in the right way. It can be the inability to discover the need to be adjusted and to amend one's way to be attuned to the development. It has to do with the nature of the deficiencies in the thought of the men that has made the irregularities in the world yet to be resolved and have solution. It can simply means the act of being undervalued compares with the intention that make one to be in the authority. It is a state at which one or government can not see beyond their immediate benefits. It is said to be the inability to look beyond one's immediate concern and issues. It is the act of not taking the others into the full consideration at the point of decision making. When one does not understand his importance in the world, it can be mental deficiency or poverty. When blames are consistently shifted from someone to another, it is often termed to be deficiency in the mental configuration. Inability to make decision that can liberate one from bondage or contribution that can lead the world in diaspora to the height of no limitation is called mental poverty. Constitutes of greed and embezzlement is termed to be mental deficiency or mental poverty.

Creation of the unnecessary fear of unknown and timidity or uproar can be termed to be mental poverty. Changing of personal definition as a result of material persuasion and influence can be defined as mental deficiency or poverty. Inability to be configured or learned on the best way of managerial concern to transform the instability in the world to capability can be ascribed mental poverty. Deformity and misconstrue of the good ideas and innovation or bringing the developmental attention to halt can be taken to be mental poverty or deficiency.

Hypocritical reasoning and decision can be termed to be mental deficiency and poverty. This is when one can not see clearly of the accurate justification in thinking for the possibility and looking into the issues around that can generate a qualitative living and economic improvement.

Applying of the theories of the nation without minding their effects or the negative implications and adverse effect can be termed to be mental poverty or deficiency. I explained before hand that, there is never any issues as regards integrating the theories around the world in the economy or in one's immediate economy, but there is always the need to determine the workability of such a theory to know if it worth it to be implemented not to cause a haphazard effect.

Thinking of the impossibility is a sign of being inflicted with the mental deficiencies. There is nothing in life that should be termed as impossible when one is fully set to be part of the activities that should create the possibilities. However, when there is a sign of complexity to understand the possibilities or to know that when issues are tackled, they are resolved amicably when one does not relent and give the adequate investment of tactics and strategies that should turn such impossibilities to possibilities, it means mental poverty.

Inability to understand the essentiality of the advantages ahead of the others, this means the inability to see the comprehensive detail of the advantages in the midst of the abnormality. It is a critical stage at which instability and other difficulties prevail in the economy, but yet, very needed for one to have the clarity of thought to be able to achieve the normality or to encourage the others within the system to have the greater access to the school of thought that can serve as remedy to the predicaments.

Being mentally and knowledgeably declined or deficient means being unable to understand the logics around leadership and representative when one is either elected or appointed/ being a follower. There are thousands of the leaders and appointees that have turned themselves to the smaller gods, forgetting that their job function is to serve the masses, being mentally deficient or poverty might never allow the leader or delegate to think straight or to comprehend on the job function or obligation that had really formulated their necessity. These and more other deficiencies are very expedient to be cross examined at the point of looking into the mental imbalances and defects.

However, poverty is poverty irrespective of its nature, but sometimes it is very advantageous to live with the poverty of having no money than being in the stage or position of not being advantaged of the efficiency in the mental condition which is therefore termed to be mental poverty.

Abject poverty can be converted when one cares to have a remedy to it, but no form of related poverty can be exterminated without being at the right state of mind. It will however be an aberration to consider the material poverty before looking into the mental poverty. When one is enclosed in the abject poverty that is in relation to material nature, he can be assured of its extermination and remedy most especially when he is fully set to make a solution to the issue at hand, whereas, mental poverty might be the greatest killing strategy to the world.

This means that, when mental poverty is the subject of the order, there is impossibility of having solution to the issue of poverty, which without doubt will definitely lead to the disability in the material, efficiency and mental nature of compositions.

CHAPTER (SIX)

<u>REMEDY TO POVERTY</u>

There is an assurance to the deficiency in the world, there is a great thought emanating from time to time to have solution to the sarcastic nature of life. Actually, if the world is not loaded with the series of the issues that are meant to be considered and to find a lasting solution to their immediate predicaments, there might not be any need to think vastly. The vast thinking of men have emanated as a result of the series of the issues that are erupting from time to time, and the consideration of looking out for the best option and solution has made a lot of propounded theories and school of thought . Most of the solution consider here are centered on the logically consideration of the real remedy. However, I will take my time to explain them one after the other briefly.

- **Logicality**- the issue of logicality is very expedient at the point of looking into the adjustment that can contribute immensely to the control of the abnormality in the world. To be able to get the authentic and acceptable standard for the control of the poverty or hardship in the economy, there is need for both the governance and individuals to be set for the logicality of existence. Logicality can be expressed in the context of matching different thought that can work interrelated. These are the systems that are combinable and which can be incorporated into each other for the purpose of making a genuine result that can affect the world at large positively. To be logical, one must be able to determine the thought and resources that can work together and the ones that can not be merged together, however thereafter, to have all it takes to be informational to have a conclusive attention and outcome. Logicality is quite very important to have a constructive nature of decision that can ameliorate the tensed situation of both mental and material poverty.

- **Creativity**- being creative means that one can come forth with something so precious within his heart, view or action. It can be seen as being extractor or excavator of uncommon ideology and terminologies that are fashioned to ameliorate the complexity in the society or the world at large. It has to do with the diversification in the thinking to come with a separation ideology with full substance that can constitute a radical change in the situation around the world. Creativity has made the improvement in the technology and other areas of life related issues very visible and to the great extent to create room for the world enlargement and total increase. Hence, creativity is very relevant to the factors that constitute transformation in the aspect of the abnormality in the society, and there is no way poverty issues as regards both mental and material can be ended without the inducement of the tactical appliances of creativity.

- **Hardworking**- to be able to get to the end of the poverty and hardship in the economy, there is need for both the governance and the populace to be industrious and hardworking. Hardworking means an attribute that is not in correlation to laziness or indolence. It is a situation whereby someone is engaged under must as a result of being compelled by the internal factors to constitute his economic contribution to have a genuine quota to contribute in line with what can bring about the economic benefit. It has to do with making things that are not working or ordinarily supposed not to work, working under the influence of one's participation and influence.

What I am trying to say is that, to end up poverty or hardship in the society, there must be disposition that understands the essence of working out the miracles and mysteries in the work. An indolent nature of human being might not be able to determine the greatest expectation in the midst of absurdity or look into the result that can be extracted as a result of not having the adequate effort that should make difference with what he has. Therefore, to be able to live ahead of poverty, there is always the need to be industrious and hardworking, because it is only hardworking human beings and nature that can over-speeds the poverty constraints and hardship.

- **Positivity**- living with the positivity aspect of thinking and action to attain purpose is quite very essential to make the world of possibility. To have a positive mind means that one has the imagination of all what it entails to accomplish a certain purpose or the other. Positive minded grow the result and outcome before they manifest or take place. They are often being controlled by the things they can see and influence from within. They are concerned and connected with the factors that are substantial and worth enough to invest on. They often know the direction of their involvement and they give the very best to make it to work accordingly to arrive at their conclusive end. They access what they need with what they can see or think, because it is already a completed assignment. They find it impossible to return back on their action as a result of their insight to see the end result or effect of their action and inaction. To then have a redress on the level of poverty or hardship, there must be sense of possibility to engage with the obligation and duties that can make it evident and visibility.

- **Courage and boldness**- living above poverty entails having the courage and boldness to make the attempts that should nullify it. When there is no courage and boldness, what is well known which should connote the solution to the poverty might be too difficult to be established. There are a lot of solution and ready made provision for answer to the difficulties, but yet, there is no courage or boldness to take the step that should lead one to the attainment of such decision and attainment. There is need to be courageous and bold to have all it entails to have the end result that should give the very best outcome. Without being courageous or being bold, having the capability to live an audacious life might be very difficult if not impossible. **Boldness and courage** are very quite necessary to have a meaningful end result that can make a logical outcome and must be into full establishment to have total adjustment on the height of the poverty and to make a resounding solution to it.

- **Directional**- to be directional means being able to walk towards a direction that can yield a definite result and which can be a beneficial to the world standard and improvement. When one plans to go on a journey, he must have a direction towards his bearing. There must be a specific direction that must be followed to achieve a particular end result. When a wrong direction is the order of one's priority or concern, it becomes very difficult or impossible to make a meaningful end result. There must be direction under must to be able to accomplish anything in life. To be directional means that one knows where he is going or has the paraphrase of the whole lots of the content of where one is heading to. Accomplishing a desire entails being encompassed with the full detailed of directional purpose that can lead one to his specific destination. To be able to find a lasting solution to the issue of the hardship or poverty then, there must be a perfect direction that should be able to tackle the delinquencies or defect appropriately.

- **Visionary**- being visionary means being possess with the vision that should make a project to work out as designed. To have vision means a strategy to accomplish task or purpose. It can be said to have direction loaded with series of factors that must be experimented in accordance with the stated program or defined procedure. It can be said to be an avenue to access the decision and authority with the foresight that was primarily designed to be attained as proposed. It can be said to be an outline for the registration of an intention. It is an arrangement that is made to accomplish its purpose at when due to the suitability of its primary structures. Therefore, to be well noted and to be able to step up ahead of the poverty or hardship, there is all need to be inclusively in alignment with the vision that can translate the whole scenario around to make an exclusive difference. There might not be any variation or improvement in the context of the absurdity and awkwardness of the poverty when the vision is not adequate and alright to meet up with the stated option to exterminate it. Hence, visionary as a means of confronting and conquering the whole delinquencies of the poverty can not be over stated to be part of the way ahead.

- **Independence**- being independent means being self reliance and totally in full control of both the physical and mental situations. It means a habit that can grow independently without minding the situation around it. It means the decision to understand that without every other condition that are necessary to make a full contribution to the existence, one still believes in the possibility and the rightful outcome that can bring about the whole nature of its desire. Independence means being able to handle situation by oneself or to take full control of the situation around his world. It means the ability to have what it entails to understand the whole logics that lead to accomplishment of purpose and getting over the issues of life. It means being audacious to mandatorily have a conclusive action that should make the list of the provisions and the worth around it to have the ending that is adequate to meet with the necessary rectification of the imbalances of the world. It is having the right order to assume the provisions that must be in control of the other conditions that should bring normalcy at all cost. These are the sets of the ideas that are labeled to be part of what prompt total freedom and liberty to assume the height of making decision voluntarily. Therefore, to have an end to the poverty and the world of hardship, there is always the need to be very self independence and to be in control of the actions that lead to the fulfillment without hesitation of what the repercussion resolved to be. Independence is one of the cultures to the outright total control of the liberty to have a pedestal that can yield the full result in the context of ameliorating the whole life in its context.

- **Fast learning**- fast learning means being able to take into cognizance of the diversified advantages one live with. Being able to see the need to have the full usefulness in the whole lots of the activities that the nature got to offer. It means being able to interpret life to its distinctive advantages and to understand the time to time requirement of existence that can translate to the high level of the worth of the advantages that should stand as catalyst to the improvement of the world in the whole classification and description. To be fast learning is to be able to read through a situation and to be able to give a definite interpretation which is not assumption but of the best antidote to the fulfillment of vision. It can be said to be a habit to be able to think vigorously to form an opinion or to be able to access the whole lots of the clues and genuine information that are embedded in the logics and fundamental reasoning. It has to do with how smart one is in term of yielding and resolving the action that has to do with the creation of vacuums within a certain decision. Fast learning means the ability to think ahead. It means the ability to see beyond the immediate issues in which one is encamped. It means the competency to reproduce within the scenario created or a problem formulated. It is the determination to see beyond the immediate lapses and conditions. To be a problem solver or to have remedy to the diversified situations of the world, there is always the very need to be very fast learning to see the conclusive end at the very initial stage of the word problem.

- **Conversion of problems or activities to benefits**- in the world, there are numerous issues that are living with men. Immediately an issue is exterminated, another issue emanates. There were issues before we were born, and there will continually be issues from time to time till the world is no more. The best of the decision to rule the world can be generated in the best issue that can be resolved. Issues are meant to be resolved at when due to be able to have the nature of the environment that can permit the full activities that should germinate the efficiency to living. Issues are always the lead way to the solution of the world, and sincerely, without being able to understand what it is to have solution to the issues, it might be very difficult to have a certain conclusion or definite result. However, to be able to have the expected benefit in the context of the condition around the world or around oneself, there is always the very need to be very enthusiastic and passionate about the conversion of the world issues and conditions to one's benefit. Whoever that is of the motive to have the benefit of converting issue to advantages must never be intimidated of the processing that leads to such end result. Issues to be rectified, served or termed as benefits must never be acclaimed problem, but a tool to attain the greater height of performance to acquire the greatest result. Hence, the ability or disposition to making the relevant issues the best factor for the major benefit must be well inclined with in the procedural attempts that lead to achievement.

- **Understandability of the time frame of the issues**- I just concluded on the fast learning and converting the issues to one's benefit. There must be what it entails to have all what it is to know of the issues that confronts one. Without being able to know that issues are never forever, there might be collapse in the construe of issues. Issues that can not be made to be understood that it can only last for the period of finding solution to them are such that might be too complex to have remedy proffer to them. To have solution to the whole conditions around humanity, there is always the need to have all it takes to understand that issues do not last forever, but might last for the time or period at which the definite solution is yet to be given to such issues. Understanding issues is what makes one to know that after the whole lots of the storm or calamity that might be as a result of an issue, there will definitely be time of stability. Understanding an issue makes one to have the nature of preparedness and relative solution that can access the issues from it in-depth to translate it to the favourable condition that can make a logical relevance in the world. However, when an issue is understood, there is always the tendency of having a solution to such issues because one can easily identifies that they are meant to be an opportunity. To however be able to overcome the unpalatable situations around the world, most especially, the issue of poverty and hardship, there is always the need to be able to understand what it is to pass through issues and to have the lasting solution to the form of the issues either materially or mentally.

- **Limitation to the economic and monetary benefit**- there are some cases that the value of the economic and monetary benefits are not to be fully considered. There is need to be able to start up a vision without the economic and monetary benefit to be outstanding and exceptional. One must be able to note that sometimes, the whole lots of the resources, time and life should be spent and validly given without hesitation for a mission to be attained. Living is very quite expedient, but living the right living is quite more very essential at the context of arriving at the greatest realm of the order of functionality. To then have a full concentration on the benefit of the intention, there must be extreme need to have a time and resources to waste. Prudential wastage or trial is never lavishness or imprudent, but the way to expand the degree of the provision of the efficacy of the valuable trait and human composition. However, there is always the need not to be too concern on the benefit of the economic and monetary benefit to be able to assume to the height of the global standard, and to make a move that other forces can not interrupt or disrupt. To move ahead of the poverty or hardship, one mind must be well positioned to know that at the very first instance or elementary stage of the life of a decision or attempt, there might be prudential investment which might never attract any form of benefit, but thereafter lead to the highest best standard that can make the world to be in the light of what you carry.

- **Exposure**- there are numerous of those who I have met with in life that have not been to school or the four corners of the class room, but yet they can perform exceedingly than some of those I know that have been to the school both locally and international. This is the result of being informed or being able to access the information that can make them to be well pronounced. One's level of exposure is concurrent with his standard of performance in the aspect of life that has to do with the logics to make an effect or impact. Impacts are made by the human based on what they can access from within, and what you can access is formulated by what you can see, while what you can see is as a result of what you know, and what you know are the things that have made you in term of what you have read or taken into consideration around you. Learning is a skill that is quite very expedient to see clearly and widely of what it entails to make transformative life or effect that can add value in holistic. Reading of novel and other text are very essential to have all what it entails to have the rightful information and insight that can be a genuine set up standard. Therefore, what you are exposed to in life is as the result of what you have made yourself to know and what you can make out of the information generated. Being exposed means the ability to see beyond your immediate environment while you have not travelled out. It means a mind or logics that are made or framed for the amelioration of the condition of the world when one is never travelled even out of his environment. It means the ability to thing largely on the circumstances that can be affect the world without being biased or having a dim thought. Therefore, being a total freedom minded personal or to have the completeness in the context of eradication of the poverty or hardship, there is always the very need to have the nature of the exposure that can make one to distinctively see and to act accordingly.

- **Informational and sensitivity**- to be informational means to be receptive and to be sensitive to the notions that are relatively available to constitute transformation at all cost in the view of the factors that are embodied to the reality to make the instance of one's option to be established. Informational means being loaded and encompassed with the due mental factors that are necessary to improvement. To be informational means that one is prone to the series of the data and insight that can cause the series of the components in the human to be adequately functional and effective. When one is informational, he can see the whole idea attributable to the concept under discussion and at the same time look into the other nature of factors that are not distinctive or directly pointed to in the line of the examination or consideration. To be sensitive means to be cautious and receptive of the impulses around one. It means to be inclusive in the thinking to extract the best outcome that can bring an upgrade at all cost to the imaginable areas of life. However, to be informational and sensitive means to be well and intact to know the varieties of the options and to evaluate them accordingly in order to have the kind of the prestigious wealth of result that can make difference in the world. To then be able to move ahead of the poverty and hardship, there is crucial need to be involved in the reasoning that has to do with being fully informational and sensitive to the circumstances around and within to make a better and most appropriate decision that can affect the world in holistic.

- **Versatility and adaptation**- being versatile means being able to convert logics or activities to such action that can bring forth a reasonable result. When one is flexible and adaptational in his disposition and inclusion in the life related issues, it means he is flexible and adjustable to make scenario around his involvement a greater privilege to make a resounding ending. Being adaptational and versatile to the issues around the world is quite very expedient to be a winner. One should be able to conceive all issues around his destiny a way to his glory, and to be able to change the activities around to their best way or usage. It means the attribute that makes the wrong to create the very best expectation, and the inhibiting values to be substantial to create opportunities. There is no way one will not see the essentiality in transforming the irregularities to the decision that should create a new world and he will be able to have such fulfillment. Being versatile and adaptational means to be able to see the whole lots of the benefits hidden in the irregularities and the capability and ordersity to make them in their best use to come forth with the best result that can create a better nature of fortune to the existence in whole. Therefore, being versatile and conversional means a lot at the point of looking into the direction of having a permanent cure to the hardship and difficulties that might be existed as a result of poverty.

- **Management of time**- one of the most difficult resources that must be critically examined and given the best of the attention in order to have the best result in any nature of the endeavors is the management of the resources that can not be renewed. There are some resources that are renewable and that can be re-generated at when due, but time is never enclosed in such a circle of the order. To be able to make the proper time management means to be able to do the right thing when due without the wastage of time. When what someone supposed to do is shifted to be done at another time, what should be done at the time slated for the intention before hand will definitely be impaired and distorted; when time is not well managed, it becomes very tedious to be relevant to the instances that can make progress or bring about the development. Managing time is very critical to be able to achieve accordingly. Where time is not managed, vision and foresight become very difficult to be attained. Things are done without being too cognizance of their time frame. Sincerely, anything without time frame is such activities that might not be too important to be considered or achieved as a result of not being adequately set to have its finished demonstration of the value that one attempts to accomplish. One of the killers of the destiny and inhibiting factors to have a better nature of innovation and the kind of the younger generation that should stand within the gap of making the moves to bring an end to the world issues is the inability to attend to the management of time. Many leave what they should do or learn for future intention, going around to waste time on the irrelevant nature of things. I have some sets of the individual around me who can not do without being involved in chatting with their friends on the phones. This often makes them more engaged in chatting other than being involved in every other nature of circumstances that should add genuine value to them. Considering the sets of the individuals that have the flare for the football also, many in my surrounding find it very comfortable to view the matches other than doing every other developmental involvement. I was trying to explain myself as regards my first book "do not be hindered by the limitation around you" to some individuals. The whole logics in the book are explaining the necessity to be a time creator. When I was in the banking sector; I often give series of flimsy excuses of not being able to attend to functions or activities or the other, whereas I could have combined series of things together. One is under must to suppose to give the very best of himself to the work he does, but that should not be the reason for being a failure. A failure finds it very inconvenient to make decision that can create opportunities within the scope of his operations. While diligently working for an organization, thinking of your days ahead or responding to the basic necessity of life should never be a worrisome or not attending thing. Out of no time, there must be time to make little impact in your capacity. While I was in the banking hall, I should have started writing my books gradually, which means by now, I would have seen myself with better outcome or result and have moved beyond the state at which I am. There must be reasonable management of time to be able to ascertain a clearer future. There must be appropriate scheduling of programs to meet with the standard that can make a perfect functionality and completeness of thought. To then be able to ascend above the drought and difficulties of hardship and poverty, there must be structure and human nature that should understand perfectly of the importance of the time management.

- **Resilience**- being resilience means being able to develop elastic nature of behavioral concept and dynamics. It means one can bend, be bent and yet, he can stand up appropriately without too much of being affected by the kind of the system he passes through. It can be a dynamic attitude to condole the whole effect around the undertaking and being able to stand in the midst of the pressure to take full control or to take charge. One of the most necessary natures that a human being must posses is to be very resilience. As time changes, so also the various kind of the activities in the world. Irrespective of the changes and nature of the types of the confrontational issues, there is need to be dynastic and to be stable to resolve it. To be able to have solution to the stubborn issues in life, there is every need to be stubborn minded entity. However, being a stubborn minded person to have a lasting solution to the issues of the world, most especially the one in relationship to the issues of poverty and hardship, there is always the very important need to be resilience.

- **Continuous learning**- to be engaged in continuous learning means to be expended for the constant learning. Being available to add value at all cost to one's personality. Willingness to acquire knowledge and to know more of the things that are not known by someone before hand. It can be said to be friendly with the academics and technical aspects of life. It is a measure at which one decides to learn of the things that are not learnt or understood. It is a situation at which one understands the value attributable to having more insight in the knowledge that emerges the world development. Age is never a barrier to the continuous learning, because it is one of the most crucial aspects of living that determines one's end result and interprets the level of one's maturity. The more one learns, the more his thinking efficiency becomes. There are some rationale that are not determined by any definition or standard that can be accessed or determined through being exposed to the nature of the standard knowledge either in a formal or informal ways. Therefore to overcome the issues of the hardship, there is crucial need to be engaged in the continuous learning.

- **Connection with the appropriate standard and quarters-** being connected means being able to get affixed with a particular source or system. There is need to be well connected in term of the standard and the categories of the set of the entity that are required to be part of the success story of a project. The standard of a vision can be evaluated in its acceptability or the yardstick that is often given to measure the level of the acceptability of a service or product. While when one is looking at the quarters that are meant to exist to constitute the best outcome, one can cross examine the nature of the bodies or group of organization that are meant to be an assisting engineering support to the vision. To then however be able to live above poverty or ahead of poverty, there is always the need to be adequately connected with the right standard and to be able to understand the series of the quarters that are responsible for the better performance of the marketing strategy of the services and commodities. This is one of the major elements that must be thoughtful to be able to outlive poverty.

- **Simplicity**- to be simple means to be able to consider things with simplicity and matured mind. It means being too easy to note that anything as issues arise must be resolved. It means being able to identify issues and knowing that they are meant to be part of the assembly of the opportunities to create a better standard and better world. It means the ability to understand that if at all things are not in order; they can still be very adequate to meet with the standard to have the best result. It can be said to be the ability to grow in the various circumstances and to react to the opportunities when they are visible or not. It is a nature that goes with not minding to go low to grow from the lower stage to the highest level. It has to do with blending up with the situations around human to create a better nature. However, to be able to meet up with the standard that got to do with the amelioration of the poverty, there is very expedient need to be simple in nature. Without simplicity, something that is not cumbersome at all might be pronounced totally unattainable or too difficult to attempt.

- **Focus**- it is very possible one got a very adequate vision without being focus. One can handle a situation that should yield the very best result with the strategies given, but without focus, nothing can be accomplished. To be focused means being able to have a simple thought of consistency and perpetual action. Since the vision and all the other strategies are made up by the human nature, there is every tendency to have changes on them from time to time, most especially, when the result or the outcome are not as expected. To be focused means that, if at all there is any crucial need to amend the nature of the projection and vision at hand, the mind set to accomplishing the stated vision should not be hampered or changed. To be focused means to be unswerving and very consistent on the end result of a foresight and making all necessary effort to make the factors provided for the attainment of the foresight to work interrelated to bring out the designed optional end means. To be out of the cage of the poverty, there must be vision that is backed up by the full focus to the attainment of the decision.

- **Discretional and decisional**-I must have said something about being independence before now. One of the major tools to be able to live above poverty is both mental and physical independence. There might never be any room for one to be discretional or decisional without being independence. To be discretional means to be able to take decision or handle situation without the prior knowledge or too much of concern of the others. It means being able to see beyond what others can see as regards the situation that has to do with someone to be specific. It means the actions and the efforts that bring out the best of the human values to handle or to take control of unpleasant and mostly odd situations. They are the decisions that are taken either consciously or unconsciously to resolve the issues that could have generated a greater havoc or destruction. Being discretional or decisional is very vital to be able to cross over the instance of poverty or hardship.

- **Exceptionality**- every man were born in an exceptional manner. The work of creation made it very easy to interpret the peculiarity in men. If all men were born to demonstrate different function and activities, then, there is need for all to function at the point of his requirement or necessity to be able to attain exceptionality. Being exceptional means to be able to segregate oneself in term of efficacy and effectiveness. It means being able to lay down standards that are not common but in relation with common sense. It means the ability to demonstrate the essential value that should be worth enough to make the nature of the contribution that a man is made up to be exhibited. It means to be distinct or unique in the systematic approaches or tactic to accomplish the issues in relation to the existence and the activities therein. To curb the power or instance of poverty therefore, there must be a thorough mind that knows its essentiality, and that is willing to make sure that such nature or essential value are quickly identified to be of greater use for the advancement purpose and to separate oneself from the multitude. Without being exceptional, the world can not be exceptional and there might not be an avenue to demonstrate the essential worth of men to take them to places.

- **Hypothetical and practicality**- to conclude on being hypothetical and practical means that something possesses the nature that can translate intention to the visible and adequate values. It means having the impact of the vision in life or demonstrating the whole logics of the intention to suit purposes. It is a situation at which reasoning and thought are graduated to the activities and actions that are meant for their establishment. It can be said to be application of the theoretical worth or values. It is the conversion of the information and it processing to the attempts of rendering solution to their intention of being formulated or essence. However, to be successful minded or be able to get over the unwarranted circumstances of life, there is always the need to be able to convert the intention to reality statement. One must be able to see the solution to the whole lots of the issues present in the world, and at the same time be able to put them into the full action to resolve such issues.

- **Result oriented**- Being result oriented means that one is of the motive to have a result under must irrespective of the challenges or difficulties that one might go through at the course of accomplishing a task. There is no task that does not have one thing or the other as impediment at the point of attempting to bring them to conclusion. Issues are part of the major ingredients to have a dependable and sophisticated outcome, and they must be well planned, analyzed, interpreted and applied to be able to have a full completed action that can lead to the desirable options. However, to be well nurtured and to be full of expectation on the result on any of the activities that one might be willing to consider, there is always the need to be result oriented minded. This means that one is of the position of the mind that can see the result of an act irrespective of the circumstances or the nature of the imbalances. It means the act that makes provision for its futuristic end expectation. One must be lined up where the optimistic nature of mind set operates to be resulted minded. It can be said to be making the possibilities in the midst of the impossibilities. To however be very result oriented means a lot to be able to cross over the torture of hardship or poverty.

- **Divine direction**- being divine directed means that one is in connection with the things that are unseen. There is no one that is not wired in such a manner to be able to connect with the things that can not be seen, but in association with the great fortune when they are accessed. To be connected at the realm higher in the spirit means having the advantage over the disadvantages around. When one listens to his or her inner self, he can see better and clearer of the things that are physical. The starting points of greater things are in connection with what one can access from within. To be an achiever or successful entity, seeing the logicality of achieving greatness form within must be a priority. However, to have a control over the situations around, there is always the crucial essentiality of being divinely directed.

- **Never settle for the less**- settling for less means accepting life the way it has come to one's way. Believing in the circumstances and misfortunes as if they are made to be destiny. Thinking that there can never be remedy to the issues at hand. Looking into the problems as if they are being inflicted rather than being emanated as a result of what were not done. Not knowing that the challenges that are won are challenges that can lead one to better height. It means thinking that opportunity lost can not be regained. It means the inability to give out something prestigious to gain the full control of one's life. It is a situation of offering oneself or selling oneself, his ideas and total dreams for the sake of being able to live. When one settles or often settles for less, he often finds himself more in a cumbersome situation. Having oneself in a tight situation is never a sin or a crime if only one understands the whole lots of the benefits therein if he can be able to compose a strategy that can cause its translation. However, settling for the less is never the antidote to freedom, but it is a measure to the complicated situation as a result of being afraid to fight the battle to win. Timidity and cowards are often of integral part of failure. They are translated to be no one as result of what they can not resolve or proffer simple remedy to attain. However, being on a hot seat does not mean that it will persist forever if there is thorough planning and structure to have solution to the situation. At the point of having a challenge or the other, intuition should be able to continuously repeating it that, it is possible to have a better ending in the midst of the greater life's challenges and not to attempt to be undervalued to bring forth the prestigious end result. Therefore, to be ahead of the poverty, there is ultimate need to never settle for the less, but for the best.

- **A thinker of developmental values-** a thinker of the developmental value can never be poor because life is composed of the various issues that must be resolved, and these sets of the issues give birth to the various areas of functionalities of the individuals. Without being able to distinctively discover one's need in the relative issues around the world, there might never be any means to be an achiever in any way. Having something to be added as value means that one is not empty, and if one is not empty, he can never be empty in real life, because someone must just be in need of what you have to offer. However, to be a champion or to live above poverty, one must be able to think supernaturally to be able to add value under must. There must be something that one discovers, and it must be well invested on to be a catalyst to a better existence which however translates to what will automatically affect the financial efficiency and capability.

- **Must be less concerned about distraction**- being distracted can be an ailment to the detrimental values that can destroy the importance of human nature. To be a growing vessel and to have a definite accomplishment, there must be a total full concentration to the achieving of a set goal. There are always different categories of distraction that are visible at the point of being a predecessor of success. There can never be a champion without being a failure or learning at a point in time. However, the stages that are required to be formulated or made are very relevant to become one's desire and must be well managed. There will definitely be distraction of a kind or the other to be formulated. But to be a successful minded or individual, there must be control over all nature of the circumstances that can be extermination to the logics of creativity and innovation. Looking into the distraction or side challenges is quite very hindrance that can make no vision to work accordingly. Therefore, to live over the issue and challenges of all sorts in which poverty is not exempted, there is need to be able to live above all distractions or side effects that can extinct one's ambition.

- **One must be involved and engaged**-being involved or engaged means being able to have interest in a particular field of studies or rationality. It means an act of being very concern about the affairs of the environment or things that can be accessed. It is an act of looking into the matters other than cross examining them without a genuine basis. It is an involvement in an operation that leads to either success or failure, but the chief concern of this book are those things that translate to success. It can be said to be an act of being in charge or in authority to take some drastic decision that should be the set of the value added to the already made decision. Before one can study the book" ahead of poverty" collectively, extensively or in conglomeration, the studies must be extended to the individuals first. To nullify the poverty or hardship, there is every need to be adequately involved and engaged. Quite so pathetic that, most the populace have the concern to have a lasting solution to the word" hardship" but they are yet to be very available for the purpose to end it up. Having a solution to the world issues means having interest in giving the relative solutions and remedy that can stand as corrective measure to the menaces. Issues might not be resolved without the full participation of the human or the total attention of humanity. The sets of the issues that are resolved are labeled to be part of the issues discovered and worked on to have their remedy. Therefore, looking for the best option to the amendment and restructuring of the various activities around the world is always in connection with the attitude to resolve the termed issues amicably. To have a lasting solution to the hardship and poverty, there must be involvement and engagement which can not be separated from that of human beings.

- **Responsiveness**- to be responsive means to be able to react to a situation in a way or the other. It means reacting in the direction of circumstances, and balancing the logics and operations around incidences. It means prompt attention and reasoning on a spectacular instance. It can be cleverness and smartness to be part of effect. Being responsive to the issues around the poverty and hardship is however very expedient to come to the end of it. I just concluded on being involved or engaged, there is no way one will not be responsive and he will be involved or engaged. One can only be involved or engaged with the things that he can respond to. However, being responsive means a lot to the issues of being fully prepared to have a conquering knowledge on the hardship and poverty. To then achieve the word" ahead of poverty" there must be necessity to be responsive in all nature to the issues around the discourse.

- **Loyalty to the world and oneself**- what does loyalty means? It means being devoted to the service and contribution that can lead to the way ahead in the world. It means being structured or configured to make a meaningful impact or effect in life. It can be said to be an act of faithfulness on the things that are committed to one's hand either by selection, nomination, election or as a result of it being a mandatory circumstance to do such an obligation for the world's expansion. It is said to be an act of faithfulness, allegiance and devotion to one's life and the world. However, to be able to cross over to the next level of life, or to be able to activate or actualize the mission to alleviate poverty or to reduce the tense situation around one's destiny, there is always the excessive requirement to be loyal and to be faithful in one's capacity and level of operation. Without being loyal to oneself and the world, being able to determine one's place of functionality might be extremely difficult. Loyalty however is one of the bases for the amelioration and the standard of the economy. When the populace is loyal, the economy and its effects are always very friendly, but when it in contrary to loyalty, diversified issues are the subject of the order. To then have a conclusive end result on the matters in relation to abject poverty creation and eradications, there must be loyal minded individuals to make worthwhile contributions that must foster the nature of the economy of the world.

- **Struggling hard to make impact**- to make impact means to be able to formulate the strategies to be involved and engaged. Making impact in not simple in nature, taking a step that can lead the world to the next level is not easy to make when determination is exonerated. There can never be any result without investing strength, time, resources, dexterity, logics, e.t.c. These sets of the investment are very tensed to be given mostly when one is unprepared. There is virtually nothing in life that does not entail the full investment of human capacity to accomplish them. Therefore, to be able to live above the influences of the hardship and poverty, there must be an element that makes one to be very responsive to be an overcomer under must. Nothing in life is easy, but they can be very easy when they are handled with the mind set of being a champion, and sincerely, to be a champion, it means one must be able to give additional effort to do better than the others at the point of attainment. Therefore, struggling hard to accomplish is one of the factors that must be considered to be able to overcome the odds of life in which poverty and hardship is not exempted.

- **Disconnection from the mundane thought**- what are the mundane thoughts? They are the sets of the thought that are meant to be for the foolishness and retrogressive nature of human. They are associated and enclosed within the circle of the mundane minded, seeing the world at its best and looking not to make any meaningful effort to make changes around them. Mundane thought are the nature of the thoughts that are often viewed in their regular nature other than looking at the way they can be improved. They are the sets of the kinds of the thought that are counted to be ordinary instead of making them special. They are the things that are numbered to be regular routine other than looking for how they can be affected to yield their better results. They are structured around what the people can see without looking at what they can be created to do. They are the sets of the thoughts that are not developmental in their nature. They are subjected to the one way traffic decision and implementation. To be versatile and be constructional in thought and logics, one must be able to think above the mundane nature of thoughts. Being mundane on the issue of poverty and hardship means looking into the situation as if they are the best the nature got to offer. It means accepting fate other than converting situation around to its best outcome. To be ahead of poverty, there must be total disconnection and discontinuity of mundane thought to grow. There must be readiness to go miles to find solutions to the irregularities and abnormalities other than looking for the short cuts. The activities around the world are often controlled by the nature of the activities that human beings inject to the world, and the one that are natural can as well be regularized by the nature of the efficacy of the men to handle the relative situations. If that is then the case to be outstanding, separation from the mundane understanding is very necessary to be able to move over the impediment of the hardship.

- **Exposure**- to say exposure means to think of the ability to learn things that are in association with the development and advancement in the world. It is all about what one knows or what he has learnt as value to affect his thinking. It means the ability to see farther and clearly of the objectives that are associated with the transformation of the world. It means given priority to the activities that are responsible for the control of the world. Looking into the various avenues at which a particular issue is handled in the different places around the world and the series of the outcome generated. It can be said to be studying beyond the concept of one's immediate environment. It is an inclusion in the system that create a rebrand for the reasoning and making difference with what is learnt and what is created to affect the world in holistic. When one is fully exposed, he knows of the various concepts and how things are structured in various places through travelling, reading and association with the people around the world. It is necessary to be well exposed to be able to meet the standard that can be very responsible for the total increment in the whole lots of the human endeavors. When one is well exposed, he attains the height at which the very best decision is taken. It is an enabling capability to translate the little knowledge to the vast understanding and exhibition. It can be the magical power that makes the so called nonentity to be entity of substance and glory. Therefore, to be ahead of the poverty and to be mightier in structure to challenge the impossibilities of life, there is every essentiality to know the intrinsic importance of exposure and to be able to demonstrate it effectively.

- **Sense of belongingness**- having sense of belongingness means being inclusive in the whole activities that has to do with the creation of the activities and making of life that is wider than just mere living. To have sense of belongingness means that one is often in association with the dynamics and the functionalities of the series of the opportunities that can be best made to future benefits. It means the intention to be very responsive and fully set to have a meaningful contribution that can be an outlet to the demonstration of the human worth and values. It means an act of full participation in the things that are subjected to the world enlargement and expansion. It is a measure to know that without the contribution of the men, there might not be any meaningful changes. Therefore, to be at the point of influence to the world in which one lives, there is need to have the sense of belongingness that can be a catalyst to the addressing of the issues of the hardship and poverty.

- **Election and selection of qualitative and quantitative leaders**- the nature of the growth and development in the society depend on the nature of the brain and the machineries that control the affairs of the economy. When leaders are not loaded to the beam of full understanding to ensure the reality in the context of their decisions and outputs, it becomes a very tedious instance to have a flourishing and active economic performance. There must be election and selection of the set of the individuals that can see clearly to determine the posterity and viability of the world to have a better performance.

Having great leaders with the discerning knowledge of the active part of the developmental agenda and moving the economy to the extreme height without looking into their personal interest is one of the solutions to the long destroying nature of life. There might never be any meaningful adjustment when the brains are disordered or irregular. Good minded and purposeful intentions who are willing and self motivated to cause translation are responsible for the greater outcome of economic efficacy. Therefore, to have an economy that can affect the human and populace genuinely, there must be election and selection of the leaders that are suitable for the developmental intention.

- **Effective governance**- just as concluded above, there is very crucial need to have the great minded leaders to have solution to the issues of the world. So also, there can never be good governance when the leaders that make policies are not efficient or rightly configured. Being a solution to the world economy entails being able to have a good governance that can take full control of the resources that can work together to have the best result. There can not be a good feedback in the governance without being an active participation of the leaders or the elected group of the individuals. Having the good governance means, having the provision of the social and necessary amenities around for the use of the populace. When the environment and economy is conducive enough for living, there is always the better opportunity for the citizens of the country to have what it takes them to have a better expansion and attainment of their goals. A good environment brings about the necessary development ordinarily, the people have the delight to handle task that can go beyond the level at which the government operates. There is already a yardstick that the members of the society have at hand, and which they are eager to surpass. Good governance is the end result of the good implementation of great ideas and notion. Therefore, having a successful ending at all cost to overcome the danger of the hardship and poverty means having what it entails to put in place of the necessary factors that should produce good governance.

- **Living positively and being a positive influence**- to be a champion or a successful minded indeed, there is always the need to be positive. The positive minded often see the reason for them to always be relevant to the solution of the world. They are very discomfort to seeing the irregularities and problems ruling over the affairs of the world situation. To have positive mind and a positive intention often open the greater advantages to the mind to see the relevance of personal worth and the need for full inclusion. Without being positive and being of the positive influence, one might never think of the expedient need to be active to the tune of being a contributor to the circumstances around the world. Positive minded and positive influential minded are of the mind set to arrive at all cost to their destination, and to resolve the relative issues that have been living with men for years. To however be strengthened and expanded than the power of the abject poverty and hardship, there must be a mind that is always very possible and positive to have solution to the issues of life.

Poverty and hardship are very crucial instances that must be settled to have a perfect living. Therefore, to be positive and a positive influential minded, it means being well set for the assignment of exterminating the word" hardship and poverty".

- **Dissociation from ignorance-** ignorance is the greatest disease that can kill destiny and the future of an economy suddenly. Believe me or not, when knowledge of moving ahead is excluded in the economic discussion or factors to set the world free, the nature of the feed back are more deteriorating and devastating. Sometimes, people get involved in various things without knowing that they are not right.

Ignorance means the inability to determine the wrong in the action or knowing the right in an action. There is something calls intuition, it often tells human beings the justification of an action. It is the evaluation and judgmental value in the inner membrane of humanity that often encourages them or discourages them when they step into any action of any kind. Being ignorant means the inability to understand life to its fullest desire. It means inadequacy to see the need to move the world ahead at all cost with the little of your composition and inbuilt talent. Ignorant minded is however bridled with the mind that is subjected to failure, lack of justice, improper thought and thinking, lost of hope and dream, inconsistencies of all nature and mostly, the inability to step into the action that should challenge the irregularities in the world in which one lives. It means lack of not being too coordinated within oneself to take up the right decision that can affect the entire world, thinking of oneself often other than looking into how a simple action can take place to influence the entire world. It can be said to be refraining from the whole lots of the action that can translate to opportunities of all sorts to make the real agenda that can be materialistic to the posterity accomplished. To then have all its takes to be able to lead the situation around or to have a better privilege ahead of the hardship and poverty, there must be essentiality to think out of the box and being loaded with the knowledge that can make the adequate changes.

- **Qualitative education-** to say qualitative education, it means the nature of the education that is contributory and effective enough to cause a drastic influence on the issues pertaining to the development agenda of the environment. Qualitative education is a demonstrative nature of education which is always very demanding for the perfect existence and response of its nature. This is the kind of the education that is commensurable with the nature of its effect on the economic situation.

When the education is qualitative in nature, it often germinates the qualitative result which means that the issues of hardship and poverty are subjected to it and being subdued. Qualitative education creates a platform that can make every other factor to work in association with it to have the fullest of control and dramatic expression of the end result of its purpose. There is need to have a demonstration of knowledge before it can be completed in its actual sense. Having qualitative education means being able to make enough provision to the destructive nature of the elements that are prone to the development, therefore, to have a lasting solution to the issues of hardship and poverty, there is always the need to have qualitative leaders through qualitative education to have the best result of all time, most especially for the time to come.

- **Citizen empowerment**- to say citizen empowerment, it means to be able to create the nature of facilities, provision and program that are standard enough to cater for the citizens being involved in the economical issues. Sincerely speaking, the prevalent issues are subjected to the redundancy of the citizen. If everyone is made to be available to have their contribution in term of economic functionality, the effect will definitely be noticed in the kind of the economy under discussion. I related on the issue of good governance in one of the point stated, there is need to have the citizen well equipped for the nature of their assignment and intention. Most of the citizens have learnt one job or the other, but they have no means to have the necessary tools and implements in place. Vision and plight are wasted and disused. Some want to learn different types of work, but the charges or fees are always keeping them away. The government must be available to support the citizens to be able to get some certain things done. Anything that is rational to be given support must be well attended to in other to be able to access the comfort of making them reality and realistic.

Empowering the citizens often kick them into action to give the very best to survive. Most of the poorest nation and economy are often neglecting the contribution of their citizens, thinking that, they are not too expedient to add value to the economic position. When the citizens are well equipped, their innovation and creativity knowledge are often at their best use to affect their world and that in which they are. To then think of being ahead of poverty without cross examining the factor of empowerment to the citizens mean that, the economy is not yet ascertained of the resolution and remedy to the instability and to have a completed assignment of normalcy.

- **Flexibility to change**- to change means being able to translate to another level of living or to convert one's way of operations to the standard that is expected of him as human being or thing. Change means conversion from the old nature to that of the new kind. It has to do with the varieties in disposition, thought, taste, way of life, status, and anything one can think on. It means to modify or alter something not to possess its old nature or look, quality, value, importance and e.t.c. Flexibility on the other hand means being able to demystify or blend up or adapt to the situation. However, flexibility to change means the ability to adapt to the changes around one's life or issues of life. It has to do with being able to adjust accordingly to the needs and wants as they arise. It has to do with the nature of movement to making sure that life is not stagnated at any point as a result of any nature of impediment and obstacle. To however be involved accordingly and to be able to live above the poverty and hardship, there must be an attitude that can intensify into the flexibility of change.

- **Handiwork and technical work-** sincerely, the best option for the advancement of the nations and economy is the option of technicality and handiwork. To be technically inclined means to be a master mind of production of thought and creativity. When one goes through the technicality operations and handiwork, if at all at the initial stage he is not a creator of anything, the thorough exercise gone through must be able to induce the power of thought to be creative. To be creative has to do with the real life analysis and being involved with the related issues in its real sense. It is said to be involvement that entails both physical and mental contributions. It has to do with the technical skill and knowledge to manifest thought and desire. To be ahead of the poverty as a nation or individually, there is always the very essentiality to be rightful involved in the activities that can make amendment on the initial structure and at the same time create alternative when due to serve as remedy.

- **Seeing beyond certificate**- there has been issues to most of the graduates from the time immemorial as regards the acquired certificate and the importance of the certificates. I will implore you to kindly read my book titled" the economic menaces and the intrinsic values of the formal and informal education as remedy" the book relates on the expected functionalities of the certificate acquired. I have not said working with the certificate is not good, but there must be something differentiated from what the certificate can offer you which you must be willing to make provision for to be in line with your dream and concepts. When you have nothing substantial as an outcome of the certificate or schooling, it means you might have gone through school or the place of learning without knowing the intrinsic value and worth of such purpose. Education and schooling should make one to be learned enough to assume the stage of authority to be in charge of the entire components and factors that are responsible for the best to be used out of one's life or to be produced therein. I have met with diversified nature of individuals with the series of the certificates and they are as well with the bundles of talents that should have made the world to be in look for them, but the fear of the unknown and the mind set they possess as regards the certificate they have had made them to be inactive and insignificant in the society and for themselves. Relenting on the certificate might be very hazardous most especially in the nation that is yet to be fully grown or attain the stage of full productivity in the sense that, there will always be the mind set that there will be provision of work at the end of the certificated courses without knowing that only few will definitely be accommodated into the limited spaces. However, technicality and handiwork are subjected to the things that are in connection with the daily needs and wants of men. They are in relation with the issues that are in existence and which are relevant to the balancing of the rationality of the world. There can not be mystery without the adequate understanding of what bring about the term mystery. And for the mystery to be in place or to be experienced, there must be mystic minded who are branded with the creativity knowledge and intention. To however be able to access the mysteries of life, there must be eagerness to be functional in the direction of the creating the mystery to move the nations and economy ahead. Relenting on the certificate however might never be able to produce the nature of the kind of the structure that can be able to destroy hardship and poverty in quote. However, to be adequately inclusive in the related matters that have to do with the nullification of hardship and poverty, there must be the requirement to learn above obtaining only certificate, but understanding the whole essence of the certificates acquired.

- **Implementation of industrialization policy**-industrialization is an act of making industries available in the economy. It can be said to be an act of creating avenue for the enviable environment for the productivity agenda and activities. It is a measure of setting industries up in the economy to attend to the production aspect of life to be able to have a favorable gross domestic product that can make positive influence in term of balance of payment. It is an act of attempting to improve on the economic standard of the nation. To then be able to do something very meaningful as regards preparing an economy that should be able to attend to the instability in the context of economic operations, there is need to have an industrialization gazette that can be fundamental to the formulation of a competitive standard. Having this nature of structure in place, there will definitely be an effect that will definitely convert the hardship and poverty to the greatest outcome and productivity that can easily enlist the economy among the best in term of their economic desire and activities.

- **Investment into agricultural sector-** one of the tedious constraints that had been the major impediment to the economic growth ad development is inability to have the proper investment in the agricultural sector. There is a saying that, when there is food and surplus of drinks, the power of poverty is out-rightly diminished. Most of the Africa countries are very advantaged ahead of the other nations as a result of their greener pasture and fertile land. But it is quite pathetic that most of the Africa countries are suffering from the abject poverty and severe hardship. Having a full investment in the agricultural sector is one of the major concerns to the economy that needs to move over the hardship and poverty. Graduates are meant to be encouraged to go into the mechanized farming, and should be well supported till the products in the farm land germinate. As far as I am concerned, practicing farming might not stop other desires of any literate entity to materialize. Therefore, making provision for the farming or luring the younger ones into the farming system might not really affect the other purposes to be established. When there are surplus of foods there is also less tendency to the poverty and hardship. Availability of food makes it possible to have the mind and capability of thinking appropriately. When there is sufficient food, people might not be too much of concern for the money which makes them to have the right frame of mind to have a deep thought. To be well set for the eradication of hardship and poverty, there must be an active agricultural sector in an economy.

- **Discovery and use of talent and potential**- there are several talents and potentials that are wasted around. There should be discovery and use of talent at when due to be able to contribute immensely to the favourable standard or outcome of the economy. When traits and talents are undiscovered, they are buried unknowingly and not utilized accordingly. There is a saying that the best potential and talents are buried in the cemetery. There is no doubt about this fact and statement. Many talents that were unused and hidden till death comes are buried with such individuals that however mean that it must be buried with them in the cemetery. There is expedient need to be available for the best use of talents that are discovered. Talent not discovered are never of any benefit to the world in holistic, but soonest they are discovered, there must be use of such talents to be able to make the necessary impact. There is need to discover talent and make use of such talents appropriately to be able to come forth with such life that can live above the pressure of hardship of the poverty.

- **Appreciation and encouragement of the indigenous products/services-** to be able to move ahead in term of economic condition, there is always the need to be very responsive to the appreciation and encouragement of the indigenous products and services. Most of the indigenous products and services available are less preferred to their foreign counterparts. There must be education and enlightenment to make the indigenous products and services very attractive and encouraging so as to be able to produce more of such services and products and to be able to have the adequate improvement. When the indigenous products and services are made to be better than the foreign counterparts, there is always the tendency of having more creativity knowledge functional at the cost of the advantages in the production and servicing sector. But on the other way round, when there is no request for the products and services produced in the country under discourse, there is low passion to be better involved in the productivity and creativity that lead to the services. When the creativity and innovation are accepted and given the very best response by the citizens, creating and producing more and more for the use of the citizens and for exportation turn out to be greater advantage to such economy. By so doing, there will definitely be consistent stability and regularity that should adjust the economy naturally. So, when the economy is stable, there is every tendency to have a better standard of living which will definitely affect the instance of hardship and control the poverty.

- **Encouragement of investment**- I discussed about the industrialization at the point before now. To have an industrialized economy, there must be investment by both the government and the citizens. There is need to encourage the citizens to invest their money on debenture or other means of converting the money to industrialization and investment portfolio. So also, making the foreigner to invest in the country is quite very essential. Investment must at all cost be relevant in any society that has the interest in development. When the level of the investment is high, there is every tendency of job opportunities and better performance of the economy. However, when there is investment in a proper standard, there are every possibilities of living above poverty and hardship.

- **Equitable distribution of resources-** it has been noted that most of the Africa countries live their lives to constitute hardship knowingly. Most of the affluence and literate derive their delight in making living unbearable for the other less privileged. Actually, it should not be. Everyone is meant to have free part to living and to be able to live as far as they are citizens of an economy. Often, the government tends to forget its major assignment while running after the unnecessary motives that can be suspended for the welfare of the citizens. Most of the so called representatives are found collecting exorbitant amount of money that can take care of 100 families in a month and yet, they claim to be the great leaders. Well, my point is that, there should be measures to extract certain percentage of total revenue from the industries and organizations, most especially from the ones that are making huge amount of profits to take care of the less privileged and to restore stability to the economy. There must be introduction of the taxes and levies accordingly to affect the general lives. When the interest of the leaders are rested on the money and how to embezzle from the purse of the government, apart from embezzling the funds available, their interest is always on the revenues that are yet to be generated which however means that, at the point of collection, they are directed for personal uses. To be able to get it right and to be able to have the nature of the environment that can stabilize the hardship and regulate the poverty, there must be redistribution of the resources. The essence of governance is to be in-between the rich and the poor. Therefore, the major assignment of the control of the resources to address the issues of hardship and poverty can not be over emphasized. Also, allocation to the different states or region must be well attended to in a proper way to ensure that the regions at which benefits or resources are derived are not in lack of their compensation. Similarly, there must be monthly allocation that is measured in accordance to the need of the development of such state or region. When this structure is well in place, there is no doubt that the issue of the hardship and poverty will definitely be addressed.

- **Provision of short and long term loan**- loan should be available to the kind of the projects that requires exorbitant amount to be completed but are relevant based on the assessments and requirements. There are thousands of the products and services that ordinarily should take place if there is availability of fund for their execution. Many visions are squashed and extinct as a result of the non availability of fund to erect and execute them. Therefore, the government must be set to resolve the issues accordingly to be able to get the very best output out the citizens. There are tremendous projects that are fully matured and long awaiting the contribution of the government in term of making provision of funds to carry them out. Soft loans should be made available for the establishment and attainment of purposes. When loan are made available to the populace, they are better opportune to carry out their intention and to be fulfilled. To eradicate poverty and hardship, there must be consideration of the provision of loan either the short or long term loan that should meet the demand of the desire while the government still monitors the ways the fund is spent to be able to retrieve the loan back from the populace accordingly. Availability of loan can be one of the best options to the citizens to have a way ahead of poverty.

- **Acceptance of faults**- under no circumstance should anyone be counted responsible for your fault or inadequacies. Mistakes are bound to happen, but they are meant to be adjusted accordingly. Being involved in a mistake should not be a means of shifting blames to the others. One must be able to admit the defects on whatever the outcome of his action are. That makes a man a matured minded individual. Really, there are many individuals that should be of help in a way or the other, but when they decide not to be available when you are in need of them, that must never be a tenable argument or flimsy excuse to say they are responsible for your failure. To be lifted above the hardship and poverty, there must be preparedness to be at the other side of the topic of the book. Therefore, being responsible for one's action and inaction is very vital and crucial to be able to attain a meaningful level of definite standard in relation to the life's issues.

- **Political and economy stability**- when there is stability in the political and economic situation, they are directly affecting the lives of the citizens. Citizens have better time to think and to demonstrate their values when there is stability. People walk around freely and carry out their economic function without being intimidated. Foreigners are easily persuaded to have investment while the interrelationship with the other countries around the world is quite easier. Peace and tranquility travail in the midst of the political and economy stability. However, there is opportunity for the citizens to fetch for their daily requirements and to transact business that can change their status or make them to be free of poverty nature.

CHAPTER (SEVEN)

<u>CONCLUSION</u>

I have been able to discuss on the various things that are responsible for poverty and the relative solution to them. I have given various terms and definition to my competency and level of thought as regards the assignment. One thing is of importance before I round up with my conclusion, this is to inform all the readers that, reading the books is not the antidote to living a life above poverty, but being able to understand the need to put the enlisted point into demonstration. Situation can only be changed when one has a thorough mind to translate the disadvantages to the very best of the opportunities. There is no time that is too late to make a corrective step to have a redirection and working on the set of the gazette that can bring back a better nature of destiny. Destiny not planned is the destiny denied, and there is none of the destiny that is not relevant in the context of the life related issues.

As discussed before now, being in the pain or discomfort-able situation does not mean that one is living in the poverty if he has the very giant thought of translating it under must to fortunes. The word poverty commences when there is no thought or consideration of moving ahead anymore. It is developed when all hope is lost and there is cluelessness. Also, living big or having excess of resources and material resources does not mean that one is not living in the poverty if the traits that has to do with the mental consideration are not adequate.

The major constitute of the poverty in the world must be traced to the mental poverty other than the other kinds of the originator of other forms of the poverty, this is because the resources available in the world is enough to take care of the populace.

There might not be any meaningful solution to the issues of the hardship and poverty if they are not best handled in a tactical way to have the true remedy to them. No matter how rich or abundance a nation looks like, when such a nation suffers from the mental deficiencies, there might never be any meaningful influence, but rather, there will continually be adverse effect of not being rightly informed.

Every other nature of the poverty are manageable and resolvable, but when mental deficiencies is the other of the priority, there will never be an outcome of any form of good repute at the point of evaluation of the economic improvement.

When the leaders are acerbity and they lose direction, there will definitely be every tendency of the hardship and suffering that is visible in the lives of the citizens. Responsible leaders are the responsibility of the citizen during election, hence the need for you and I to be actually involved in the series of the stages that make provision for the leaders in term of electing and selecting the right ones.

To round it up, there is no poverty that can bring an end to itself without the influence of you and I. We must be able to think it right, discuss, deliberate on the way ahead, read through the various philosophical books and write up and act accordingly to the extermination or alleviation of the poverty. There is hope and there is solution, but only to those who can

easily identify it and work tirelessly
to bring them to manifestation.
Thank you for reading through my
conceptual thought.
Remain blessed.